HELLO TOKYO

*

HELLO TOKYO

*

30+ HANDMADE PROJECTS AND FUN IDEAS FOR A CUTE, TOKYO-INSPIRED LIFESTYLE

EBONY BIZYS

PHOTOGRAPHY BY BOCO

ABRAMS I NEW YORK

This book is dedicated to you, my lovely little Sandwiches, for all your constant and ongoing support. For reading my *Hello Sandwich* blog, leaving Instagram comments and likes, for coming along to my workshops, buying my books and zines, for sending sweet e-mails, and for your unfailing encouragement and enthusiasm.

Without you, this would never have been possible. Arigatou, Sandwiches!

Love Love,
Hello Sandwich
xoxo

SUPER CUTE!

CONTENTS

HELLO
SANDWICHES!

*

Welcome to Hello Sandwich world: a tiny apartment in a little corner of Tokyo that opens onto a vast expanse of creative inspiration. I'm an Australian artist, designer, blogger, and author: My daily life in Tokyo is documented on my blog, hellosandwich.jp; on social media; and now it's here in this little book you are holding in your hands.

Living in Japan has been an unexpected whirlwind with a trail of creative projects that I could never have imagined in my wildest dreams. I've collaborated with some of my favorite Japanese brands; hosted workshops at Tokyu Hands and Isetan department stores; appeared on Japan's national television station, NHK; dabbled in Japanese radio programs; and published two Japanese craft books.

I can pinpoint the beginnings of my Tokyo creative journey to one event in particular. It took place just a few weeks after I moved to Tokyo. I was very eager to sign up to do something creative, so immediately upon arriving, I applied to take part in the Tokyo Art Book Fair. It was at this event that I met Mio-san, from Japanese publishing house BNN, who had an interest in Hello Sandwich. Mio-san promptly organized a feature in a new "girls' zines" book, and from there the opportunities multiplied. Honestly, I still can't believe it when I walk into a Japanese bookstore and spot a Hello Sandwich publication. I'm constantly pinching myself to see if this is all just one big dream.

I hope you will enjoy this peek into the city that I see every day and love dearly. And if you can, please come along and visit Tokyo!

Love Love,

HELLO SANDWICH

xoxo

✖ Find hellosandwich on Twitter, Instagram, Pinterest, and Facebook.

HELLO, TOKYO

*Being a foreigner in this city—being
able to see the city with fresh eyes—
is so, so utterly inspiring*

DAILY
LIFE
＊
in Tokyo

looking for photos

I've been living in Tokyo for five years now, and not a day passes that I don't catch myself smiling at something uniquely Japanese on my travels. It might be the striped tape seal on a brand-new package of plastic wrap, the Tiffany-blue garden hose around the corner from my apartment, or a passing polka-dot truck. The inspiration in this city is never-ending. One of my favorite pastimes is wandering around the local suburbs "looking for photos," as I call it.

TOKYO CITY SCENES It blows my mind that I'm lucky enough to be able to live in this incredible city. Spending lots of time in my local neighborhood, it's easy to forget that I live in such a megametropolis! Every now and then, I love to stop for a moment and catch a glimpse of the city from a high-rise building. It's mind-boggling. Looking down over the vast city from these heights, I'm amazed that somehow I've made a life for myself among the millions of people living here.

cherry
blossom
season

SEASONS Tokyo really is a four-season city, and it's fascinating to watch the city change from one season to the next, especially in the local shops. Supermarkets sell *umeshu* (plum wine) kits and green curtain kits (to keep out the sun) at the start of summer, bamboo decorations for the new year. . . and so on. Without a calendar, you could safely guess the date with just one visit to a supermarket.

Each season comes with its own unique events. Spring brings a week or two of *hanami* (cherry blossom viewing parties) and picnics. My favorite parts of summer are the festivals: I often sit in my studio and hear the drumming of passing processions. In autumn it's time to travel to Hakone to see the changing colors of the leaves, and in winter it's time to look forward to the snow.

Tokyo is very well equipped for each season. Trains have heated seats in winter and strong air conditioning in summer. Cafés offer hot wine, blankets, and heated hand warmers in winter, and *kakigori* (shaved ice) and frozen beer in summer. No matter what the season, it's wonderful exploring and living in this amazing city.

YUKI (**SNOW**) Coming from Sydney, I rarely ever saw snow, especially not in a city environment. It's such a brilliant experience to see your city nestled under a blanket of white. On occasion, it snows where I live in Shimokitazawa, usually in February. Waking up to the quiet of a new snowfall is utterly incredible. The snow absorbs all the neighborhood sounds, and it's the most beautiful silence you can imagine. You know it is there before you peek out your window.

In February 2014, Tokyo experienced its heaviest snowfall in forty-five years. I arrived back from Kyoto on the *shinkansen* (bullet train) just in time to see it. I wasn't even able to roll my suitcase from my local station to my house. My bike was completely covered, and the following morning I could only just make out the top of the washing machine on my balcony. It was a great excuse not to do the laundry—much wiser to spend time building a snowman, right?

Whenever this happens, I head out to take photographs, armed with my makeshift plastic bag camera protector. Those special moments in the freezing cold, snapping photos, are some of my happiest memories of Tokyo life.

The day after a big snowfall, the community comes out and scrapes the snow to the side of the streets. Business owners turn these piles into snowmen, some bigger than life-size.

For this reason, February is one of the months in Tokyo that I most look forward to.

Waking up to the quiet of a new snowfall is utterly incredible.

a good excuse not to do the laundry!

combini (convenience store) life

Travel is easy when it's this fast! You can't beat the trains in Tokyo.

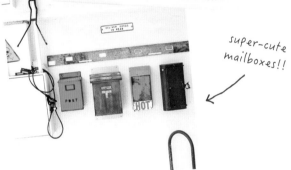

super-cute mailboxes!!

Obaachan and Ojiichan

Bisaiji-san, food artist

Mami-chan and Sophie et Chocolat

David became my "beastie" thanks to a typo I made: "love from your beastie xxx"!

David and Ros

TOMODACHI (FRIENDS) I've been so lucky to have made such wonderful friends in this city. I have to pinch myself sometimes in situations I never thought possible: sitting at my craft-book-author idol's house making miso (soybean paste), for instance; or visiting famous Tokyo-based creators Sophie et Chocolat's studio space for afternoon tea.

I have recently become friends with the family who lives opposite my apartment. I call them Obaachan and Ojiichan (Nan and Pop). They opened their home to me and often invite me to a home-cooked family dinner, water my plants for me when I travel, and cheerily greet me when we pass one another in the street. It's so special to have such a wonderful network of friends in this city.

photographer Boco-chan;
love this lady to bits

HOME STYLE

*Making good use of a compact living
space is a challenge for many in
Tokyo, but there's always room
for cute ideas*

HELLO
SANDWICH
✳
HQ

a Hello Sandwich color palette

Hello Sandwich HQ is a small apartment with a big personality!

Hello Sandwich HQ is a tiny 125-square-foot (38-square-meter) apartment in Shimokitazawa, Tokyo. This buzzy and friendly centrally located neighborhood is just four minutes by train from Shibuya (one of the most exciting and busiest suburbs of the city). The apartment is about a quarter of the size of my Sydney apartment, so it was a matter of quickly getting good at Tetris once I arrived in Tokyo. It's honestly like a little doll's house. I can almost touch the ceilings, and tall friends have to be careful when ducking through the doorway.

My corner apartment is super sunny and in a fantastic location. My landlord lives on the floor below me, which is quite comforting, and I've made friends with the local Sagawa Express and Yamato Transport delivery teams (couriers), and the post-office lady also knows me, so I really feel as though I have made a nice mark on the community here. It would be hard to leave this little apartment.

HINT

Put together assorted ceramics to make <u>artwork</u> **out of a table setting**

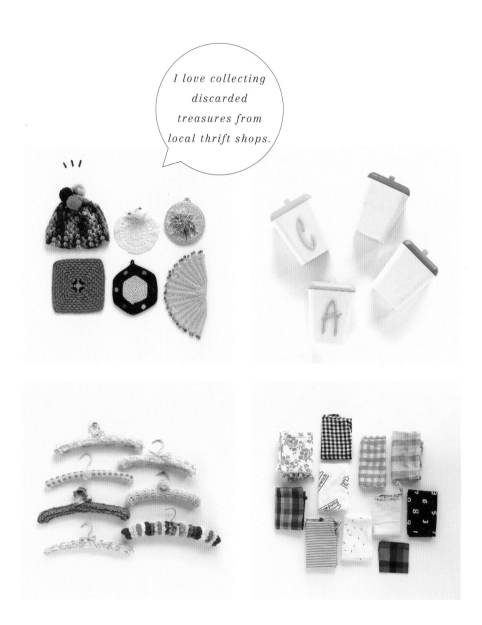

I love collecting discarded treasures from local thrift shops.

I'm an avid collector of many different types of homewares. I love scouting local vintage stores for particularly interesting treasures, especially glasses, dishes, linens, aprons, crocheted coathangers, tea cozies, trays, canisters, and colorful pot holders. When I lived in Australia, my parents had a vacation house in Culburra on the New South Wales south coast, and I absolutely adored spending time searching through the local thrift shops, finding discarded or unwanted gems. Having a mismatched serving set makes for a fun collection, and it's lovely putting together assorted ceramics and plates to make artwork out of a table setting.

*

FLOWER ARRANGING

Another thing I have noticed in Japan are inexpensive mixed bunches of flowers readily available from florists or supermarkets. I was pleasantly surprised at the reasonable price of such bunches when I moved to Japan. For a little bit of money, you can buy a colorful treat to brighten up your home.

A COLORFUL TREAT

I have a thing for short-stemmed flowers—perhaps it's because my apartment is small—so the first thing I do once I get the flowers home is cut almost all their stems off. I then spend time arranging the flowers into various combinations and popping them into assorted small vases. Generally, I separate the flowers I buy into little vases arranged by height and shape. Because my apartment is so small, it's nice to have tiny vases spread throughout the house. I have a mini single-stem vase on a wire hanger that I hang in my bathroom and another that I hang in the kitchen window. It's not uncommon in cafés in Tokyo for each table to have the tiniest vase you have ever seen holding just one sprig of flowers. Attention to detail like this has always fascinated me, and it's a part of Tokyo life that is nice to re-create at home.

FLOWER SELECTIONS It's great when your local florist offers a mixed bunch, especially if you're in a bit of a rush, but on special occasions, I go to a local flower shop at the Shinjuku train station and select individual stems of flowers, making my own combinations. I try to pick up some pom-pom-shaped flowers if they are available, some colorful flowers, and some leafy greens. I also have a soft spot for baby's breath.

BOTTLES AND GLASSES Honestly, the packaging in Japan is just so incredibly cute that it makes throwing things away a difficult task. I am guilty of buying drinks purely for their packaging, knowing they will make a great vase once the contents are gone. Try looking out for drink bottles in interesting shapes and sizes, with decorative labels, preferably in plastic. A few of the vases shown here originally contained muscat juice, *mikan* (mandarin) juice, apple juice, sake, and gin. Together, the various heights and color combinations of the bottles, labels, and flowers make a lovely little cluster.

CAN DO Some Japanese food cans are just too sweet to throw away on trash day. Instead, I keep them and use them as vases. Simply use a can opener that takes off the lid without leaving sharp edges, wash the can thoroughly, and you're good to go. You might also be able to find some retro cans at second-hand stores. The cherry can pictured above was one that I found in a little supermarket in Ishinomaki. Whenever I use it, I'm reminded of the sweet memories from that road trip.

FLOWER
TIP

4

I HEART FLOWERS I am absolutely in love with Lovestar's heart-shaped vases (see page 217). These vases come in a spectrum of colorful Perspex plastic and are handmade by a gorgeous lady named Helen, who lives on the Gold Coast in Australia.

*

CRAFT STORAGE

If you're anything like me, you might find yourself with an accumulation of craft materials that are in need of lovely homes. I've collected cute little containers, assorted boxes, cans, baskets, and canisters over my time living in Japan for this purpose.

A small portion of my masking tape collection is stored in a retro Japanese tin, while beads and pom-poms are stored in vintage cardboard boxes, colorful little clips have found their home in polka-dot plastic soap containers, and rolled papers are kept safe in a floral dustbin. Most of these containers were purchased at secondhand stores in Shimokitazawa.

I enjoy storing items in thing that were intended for a different purpose.

HINT

Most of these little <u>treasures</u> **can be found in secondhand stores**

← Schnaupi ♡

I found the wooden storage box above on the side of the road at a closing-down Japanese *izakaya* (tavern) a block away from my house. Although you can't tell from this image, it has dividers, which makes me think it might have been a box for a set of glasses or plates in its original life. The little house pen box was a present from my talented illustrator friend,

Grace Lee. The little black dog on it is a drawing of my mom's schnauzer puppy, whom we call Schnaupi (even though his real name is actually Charlie). The polka-dot tin in the middle was an antique souvenir I picked up on a trip to Kyoto. It was originally from Russia, and was used to store bay leaves.

STORAGE TIP

1

PEGBOARD! It's something you can't go wrong with. Not only is it a great storage solution, but it makes a cool backdrop for photographs. The great thing about these pegboards is that they can be customized to your requirements and can be renewed and altered as your needs change. Head to your local hardware store and buy pegboard in the size of your liking. I've used Martha Stewart Crafts Multi-surface paint and a varnish to color two of the boards.

× Use dowel rods and pegboard hooks to store the items you need to access easily.

× Attach some retro tins to the pegboard to store pencils.

× Small baskets can be added to store papers, letters, pencil packs, and so on.

*

DIY PAINTED FURNITURE

Customize your furniture with a touch of paint. The furniture items shown here were bought new, but you can often find amazing pieces in secondhand furniture stores and thrift shops. Be on the lookout when shopping for anything that could work in your current interior décor with a bit of a revamp. I found this little wooden coffee table in a furniture store in Shinjuku and painted each leg a different color to create a cute occasional table. My storage cubes were also cheap and cheerful. To customize them, and to create a colorful storage solution, some of the boxes were painted on the inside (with the front flap removed) and the other boxes had the front flap painted.

I used Martha Stewart Crafts Multi-surface paint and a coat of varnish for extra durability.

Cr. Inselsberg 916.5 m.

WILL RETURN

Pflanzenpflege
und Tiere
im Kindergarten

TOKYO
EDIT

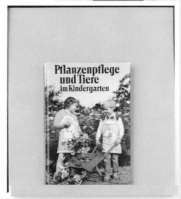

OHNÍČEK 5

ミツワ ソフト石鹸

NABISCO

PREMIUM
SALTINE CRACKERS

The cracker
that
CRUNCH.

painted plant pots

Mini potted gardens are something the Japanese do so well. Create your own green oasis by bringing the outdoors in with some potted plants. Alternatively, create a little potted garden on your balcony or other outdoor area. Here are a few of my favorite ways to customize simple, inexpensive pots.

You will need plant pots × masking tape ×
POSCA water-based paint markers × multisurface
paint and paintbrushes × spray paint × stickers × varnish

POT TIP 1

SPRAY-PAINTED POTS Create an original pot by using spray paint for a speckled or multicolored blended effect. Finish with varnish.

POT TIP 2

RETRO CAN POTS Repurpose cans that are way too cute to throw away by removing their lids with a can opener that doesn't leave a sharp edge. Make a few drainage holes in the bottom of each tin before planting.

3

STRIPED POT First, use masking
tape to mask off vertical stripes on
the plant pot. Paint the exposed area
with the multisurface paint of your
choice. Let the paint dry completely
before you carefully remove the tape.
Finish with varnish.

PAINTED POTS You can paint ceramic plant pots with multisurface paint, as I have done with the yellow pot shown here. Or try using masking tape to cover horizontal sections of the pot before painting the remaining areas with all-purpose paint, as in the blue pot with a white lip. I've used Martha Stewart Crafts Multi-surface paint.

DOTTY POSCA POTS Use POSCA water-based paint markers to draw a pattern of your choice on a ceramic pot. Here I've used a black POSCA marker to draw random polka dots on a coral-glazed pot.

POLKA-DOT STICKER POT If you have a little potted plant that you keep inside, you might like to stick polka dot stickers all over the pot. You could also use gemstone stickers or any stickers of your choice to decorate a pot that is kept away from the elements.

Do you ever receive advertising magnets in the mail? Sure, they can be useful, but they don't always look cute. My solution is to glue (using hobby glue) hand-painted patterned paper—or any decorative paper—to the magnet sheet and then cut the sheets into shapes. Half circles, triangles, diamonds, strips . . .

These can also make lovely little presents, and they certainly make keeping receipts on your fridge a lot more attractive.

You might also be lucky enough to find some magnet sheets or circle magnets at a hardware or craft store. Daiso, one of my favorite supply shops, sells cute circle magnets that I like to add to paper corsages.

HINT

These also make <u>lovely</u> **little presents**

pillowcases

Use cute printed cotton fabric to make your own pillowcases. These fit a standard-size pillow: 20 x 32 inches (50 x 80 cm).

STEP 1

You will need 74½ x 20½ inches (189 x 52 cm) cotton fabric **×** sewing machine (or hand-sewing equipment) **×** scissors, pins, needles and general sewing supplies **×** iron and ironing board

STEP 2

STEP 1 Start with the fabric facing the wrong side up. On one short edge, fold a ⅜-inch (1-cm) hem, then fold a 2½-inch (6-cm) hem. Press and pin the hem. On the other short edge, fold a double ⅜-inch (1-cm) hem. Press and pin the hem. Stitch both hems along the inside edge.

STEP 2 Lay the fabric flat with the right side up. Bring the edge with the larger hem over toward the narrow hem, leaving 8 inches (20 cm) of fabric to create a flap. Fold the flap back over the top of the layer with the larger hem, making sure the hemmed edge underneath is aligned with the crease the flap has formed. Pin the long edges of the pillowcase together and stitch through all layers with a ⅜-inch (1-cm) seam allowance.

STEP 3

STEP 3 To prevent fraying and reduce bulk, trim the seam allowance by half and use the zigzag stitch on a sewing machine or overlock the edge. If you are hand sewing, use the blanket stitch.

STEP 4 Turn the pillowcase right side out (the flap will now be inside the pillowcase) and press to finish. Insert your pillow and dream sweet dreams.

STEP 4

HINT

Be sure to wash and <u>iron</u> **the fabric before you start**

*

DOTTY TABLECLOTH

Dress up your dining table with a customized tablecloth. You can start with a ready-made tablecloth, or, if you're handy on a sewing machine or with a needle and thread, double hem a piece of fabric to the size of your choice. Trace around the inside of a roll of washi tape (such as mt tape) to mark out your dot pattern, then paint inside the dots with fabric paint. You can also use masking tape to mark off stripes or other designs of your choosing before painting.

CUTE
PROJECT

THE THRIFTY
10 yd
91 m

mismatched napkins

This easy project is a great way to use up small pieces of cotton fabric you may have in your home. It doesn't matter if the fabric patterns are different, so long as the sizes are identical and the colors work well together. You can create a fun and unique set of table napkins by double hemming these squares of fabric. I've made small napkins perfect for informal lunches and breakfasts, but you could really make these napkins any size you like.
Be sure to wash and iron the fabric before you start the project as some fabrics can shrink once washed.

STEP 2

You will need 10-inch (25 cm) squares of cotton fabrics ✖ sewing thread ✖ sewing machine (or hand-sewing equipment) ✖ scissors, pins, needles and general sewing supplies ✖ iron and ironing board

STEP 3

STEP 1 Start with the fabric facing the wrong side up. Fold and press a $^3/_8$-inch (1-cm) hem around all edges of the fabric squares.
STEP 2 Open out the ironed hem and fold in the corner diagonally as shown in the image.
STEP 3 Tuck the point of the fabric under itself and refold the ironed hem.
STEP 4 Turn the hem over once more to make a double hem and secure it in place with some sewing pins. You will find you have a neat little mitered corner now. Finish by sewing around the inside edge of the hem with a straight stitch either using a sewing machine or by hand.

STEP 4

A HANDMADE LIFESTYLE

*Small ways to bring happiness
into everyday life*

*

PICNIC

One of my favorite activities in Tokyo is to pack an *obento* (lunch box) and picnic basket and set out for the park. This simple activity involves so many of my favorite things: bike riding, friends, taking photos, and relaxing in nature. There are many gorgeous parks in Tokyo that lend themselves to an afternoon of relaxation and leisure. Call some friends, pack a few luxuries (fresh flowers, blankets, mismatched napkins, and the latest issue of your favorite publication), and spend the afternoon together in a lovely nearby park.

MUSICAL INSTRUMENTS No picnic would be complete without some beautiful musical instruments. A xylophone, Tenori-on, portable eighties record player, or even music-making apps, such as Lullatone's Patatap, should do the job nicely. On this day, David-san packed one of my favorites, Grimes, on vinyl to play on his retro portable record player. He played along with the record, making sweet little Lullatone-esque soft sounds on the colorful xylophone, setting a happy atmosphere for our picnic.

PICNIC TIP
2

ACTIVITIES In addition to music, items such as playing cards, dice, books, pencils, and craft materials are all lovely items to bring to a picnic for relaxing entertainment.

PICNIC TIP
3

PACKING FOR PICNICS Picnic baskets are always a lovely way to transport items to the location. A little extra time spent packing a small, vintage-style basket beautifully will make the food, sparkling wine, blankets, books, and other things you need look extra special once you arrive.

PICNIC TIP 4

SHOES OFF! At Japanese picnics—as in Japanese homes, where one takes off one's shoes at the front door—picnic blankets are often surrounded by a scattering of shoes. I often think just how divine and gorgeous the shoes look in a little row next to the blanket. Another fun fact: picnic blankets are often referred to as "leisure sheets" in Japan.

PICNIC TIP 5

PICNIC FOOD Food artist Bisaiji-san created these beautiful and colorful foods for this picnic. Bite-size food that is easy to eat and easy to share is recommended for picnics. Onigiri and sandwiches are favorites. And dips with crisp vegetable sticks look colorful and are healthy and delicious to enjoy in a park. Extra points for crinkle-cut veggies.

*

BENTO ESSENTIALS

kuro
(black)

shiro
(white)

kiiro
(yellow)

aka
(red)

midori
(green)

BENTO TIP

1

You might be aware of the "five color rule" that says each *bento* (lunch box) should contain at least five colors; however, you may not know that the ideal bento should be constructed according to five sets of five rules. These are:

× Five colors: *aka* (red), *kiiro* (yellow), *midori* (green), *kuro* (black), *shiro* (white)

× Five cooking methods: *niru* (simmer), *musu* (steam), *yaku* (grill), *ageru* (fry), *tsukuru* (create).

× Five flavors: *shiokarai* (salty), *suppai* (sour), *amai* (sweet), *nigai* (bitter), *karai* (spicy)

× Five senses: *miru* (see), *kiku* (hear), *kyukaku* (smell), *ajiwau* (taste), *fureru* (touch)

× Five viewpoints or outlooks (*gokan no mon*): a set of Buddhist principles on the appropriate state of mind when consuming food

I have a little "bento" drawer in my mini Shimokitazawa apartment. It's full of cute accessories that inspire me to make bento boxes: bento dividers, bento belts, bento patties, sauce containers, and *onigiri* (rice ball) wrappers.

There is another entire cupboard dedicated to *furoshiki* (wrapping cloth) used for bento wrapping. I also have a collection of bento lunch bags and bento freezer packs. When you buy refrigerated goods from fancier supermarkets in Tokyo, you often receive little refrigerator packs taped onto the cold goods. These reusable packs are great for keeping your bento fresh. You can also buy cute versions of these, such as heart-shaped coldpacks with sparkle dust inside and so on.

Many Japanese stores, such as Daiso (daisojapan. com), sell a large range of bento accessories and essentials, such as seaweed punches, picks for small vegetables, and other *obento* items.

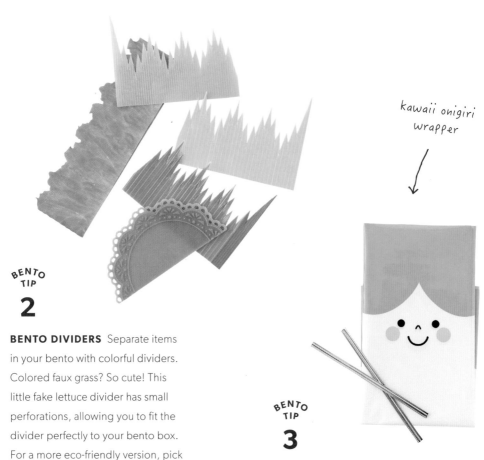

kawaii onigiri wrapper

BENTO DIVIDERS Separate items in your bento with colorful dividers. Colored faux grass? So cute! This little fake lettuce divider has small perforations, allowing you to fit the divider perfectly to your bento box. For a more eco-friendly version, pick up silicone dividers such as the lilac doily option shown above.

ONIGIRI WRAPPERS There is nothing more pleasurable than biting into an onigiri with crunchy seaweed. In order to keep the seaweed crunchy, you'll need to pack your onigiri in one of these wrappers, which keep the rice and seaweed apart. Imagine this cheery little face waiting to greet you at lunch!

BENTO PATTIES Bento patties are a fantastic and colourful way to keep your *obento* ingredients separated and fresh until you are ready to enjoy your *obento*.

Divide each little *osozai* (side dish) with a bento patty. Try mixing a variety of colors and patterns. I've found some in sweet patterns such as gingham, stripes, and polka dots. If you have a green *osozai*, such as spinach or lettuce, try using a contrasting patty for aesthetic effect.

You can also find silicone versions of bento patties, which can be reused without any reheating issues.

BENTO PICKS Bento picks can help to arrange little items—such as a cube of cheese, a small roll of ham, a mini tomato, or a pickled vegetable—and keep them in place in your bento. They also make eating these items a lot easier. The variety of bento picks available in Tokyo is enormous, but you may also be able to find some at your local Japanese market.

depachika obento

BENTO TIP

6

SUPERMARKET OBENTO A delicious and convenient obento is never too far away in Tokyo. Most supermarkets and convenience stores sell colorful and inexpensive obento at all hours of the day. Many department stores have a basement food level where you can find delicious obento. These are called *depachika obento*: *depa* is short for "department store," and *chika* means "basement." It's ridiculous just how tasty, cheap, colorful, and presumably healthy(ish) these obento are!

BENTO TIP

7

OBENTO FUROSHIKI *Furoshiki* are cloths used to wrap many objects, particularly obento. They are such a pretty way to transport your lunch, and provide a lovely little impromptu tablecloth, too. There are many types of *furoshiki* and various ways of wrapping them. In true Japanese style, there is an entire art to *furoshiki* wrapping, and you can find many tutorials on the Internet.

HOW TO ENJOY

*

eating at home

> *I love my quiet mornings in the sunshine.*

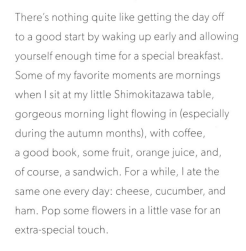

There's nothing quite like getting the day off to a good start by waking up early and allowing yourself enough time for a special breakfast. Some of my favorite moments are mornings when I sit at my little Shimokitazawa table, gorgeous morning light flowing in (especially during the autumn months), with coffee, a good book, some fruit, orange juice, and, of course, a sandwich. For a while, I ate the same one every day: cheese, cucumber, and ham. Pop some flowers in a little vase for an extra-special touch.

hello sandwich

Some of my favorite moments are when I sit at my little table.

gorgeous morning light flowing in

HINT

Pop some flowers in a little vase for an <u>extra-special</u> **start to the morning**

polka-dot tray

There's nothing nicer than treating a guest to morning coffee on a cute tray adorned with a simple bloom in a miniature vase.

You will need wooden tray **×** round stickers **×** multisurface paint **×** paintbrush **×** craft knife **×** clear varnish

STEP 1 Cover the tray with stickers, making sure to press down on the edges of each sticker so that they are firmly in place and no paint will be able to seep under the edges. I've used jumbo dot stickers, but you can also use smaller dot stickers or experiment with masking tape (masking off different shapes and areas or creating stripes or zigzag patterns for a different effect).

STEP 2 Use multisurface paint to cover the whole surface of the tray. Make sure not to add too much water to the brush, which might cause the paint to thin and seep underneath the stickers. Allow the paint to dry with the stickers in place.

STEP 3 Slowly and carefully peel off the dot stickers. Use the tip of a craft knife to gently lift the edges, if needed.

STEP 4 Apply a coat of clear varnish and allow it to dry overnight, then the tray will be ready to use. Yay!

HINT

Make sure stickers are <u>firmly in place</u> **before painting**

We dip into our handbags on a daily basis, so it's worth spending the time to find or make a few of these happy-making items: buy a cute pouch to store your makeup; splurge on a diary that will last you a lifetime; present your business cards in a case that you're proud of; keep your rewards cards organized (extra points for floral and metallic!); and buy little luxuries and necessities, such as mints and tissues, in the cutest packaging money can buy.

LUNCH ON THE RUN!

T R A V E L
T I P S
*
a road
trip

♡ ♡

Shower Cap
MAKE YOURSELF COMFORTABLE

*station
obento*

business travel ↓

For me it's a very special occasion to be traveling in a car in Japan.

Road trips in Japan are one of my favorite things ever. Whether it's travel by train or by car, it's hard to go wrong when you're on this lovely little island.

The trains are incredibly reliable and convenient. If a train is just a minute late, you can expect to hear apologies over the loudspeakers, and it's not uncommon to receive a letter for your school or work handed out by train station staff should the train be a few minutes (gasp) late. The *shinkansen* (bullet train) is a fantastic way to travel and offers an alternative to flying, while local trains allow some slow time.

Even after many road trips here, I still feel as though it's a very special occasion to be traveling in a car.

Apart from catching taxis, I am rarely in a friend's car or rental car in Japan.

When I take a *shinkansen* I love to pick up an *ekiben*: *eki* is the word for railway station and *ben* is short for obento, so literally a "station obento." These colorful little meals all neatly packed are so lovely! Once I was headed to Nagoya and found myself next to two businessmen. All three of us placed our *ekiben* on the tray table in front of us, and it was clear we were keen to open them. We joked that we should at least wait for the train to take off before we started eating.

Watching all the businessmen open their little wet towels and chopsticks—even putting their hands

collecting memories

together briefly as in prayer for a quiet *itadakimasu* (thanks for this meal) before eating—reminds me that I am a long way from Australia!

When I travel for business in Japan I often stay at cheap and cheerful business hotels. They often have the best breakfasts: miso soup, fish, rice, eggs, pickles, and seaweed. One can really get used to this way of starting the day. Many Japanese business hotels offer two types of tea (rather than coffee and tea) in the hotel room: green tea and *ume* (plum) tea. I can't help but save these little packages as memorabilia.

I love collecting anything from a trip: flyers, the tops of small milk containers, sugar-stick papers, postcards, maps, handwritten notes, *purikura* (photo booth sticker printouts), rewards cards, and so on. These little items can be collected in a folder, and if you ever return to the location, you can pack this little journal and perhaps even revisit some of the places. Sometimes looking at a handwritten note or a hand-drawn map can evoke stronger memories than the photos you took at the same location.

While traveling, I try to focus less on the tourist sights and more on the backstreets, cafés, and local people so I can really capture the essence of their everyday lives in my photographs. It's nice to find off-the-beaten-path memories to hold on to.

capture moments that
spark your imagination

CUTE
×
PROJECT

hair bow

You will need two 3½ x 8½-inch (9 x 22-cm) strips of cotton fabric ✕ sewing thread ✕ sewing machine (or hand-sewing equipment) ✕ scissors, pins, needles and other sewing supplies ✕ comb hair accessory

STEP 1 Fold the strips of fabric in half crosswise and lengthwise and cut a curve at the end as shown in the photograph.

STEP 2 With right sides of the fabric together, sew all around the edges leaving about a ¼-inch (5-mm) hem. Leave a small gap in the middle of one straight section so that you can turn the bow right side out once you have sewn it.

STEP

2

STEP 3 Cut tiny slits perpendicular to the curved parts of the seams with a sharp pair of scissors to reduce the bulk. Turn the bow right side out by pushing the fabric through the small gap. Tie the piece of fabric into a loose knot and mold it with your fingers to form a pleasing bow shape.

STEP 4 Hand-stitch the bow to the straight edge of the comb accessory, and your bow is ready to go! It would look super-cute adorning a topknot, don't you think?

STEP

3

STEP

4

HINT

Mold it with your <u>fingers</u> **to form a pleasing bow shape**

charm bracelet

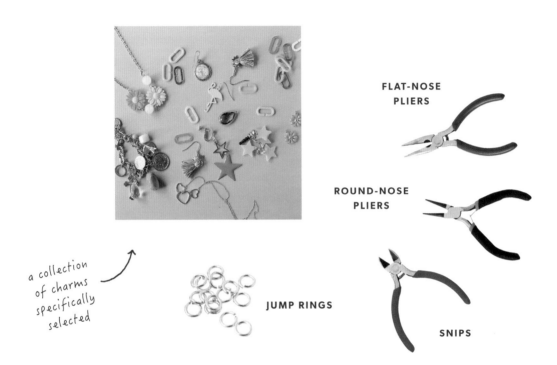

FLAT-NOSE PLIERS

ROUND-NOSE PLIERS

JUMP RINGS

SNIPS

a collection of charms specifically selected

Do you have some charms, little trinkets, or single earrings around your home that are too sweet to throw away? If not, you can buy an assortment of inexpensive charms, necklaces, earrings, and bracelets that can easily be dismantled and formed into charms. I bought these charms from various shops including chain stores. You might be lucky enough to find an inexpensive bracelet that has a nice chain and a few charms, but to make it the perfect charm bracelet with an individual style that exactly fits your taste, why not add some extra ones you've hunted down?

You will need some flat-nose pliers, round-nose pliers, snips, and jump rings. Use the snips to cut off any charms you like from existing earrings and necklaces. Next, clip off any existing charms that you don't want to include in your final piece. Now lay the bracelet out straight and line up the charms. Keep in mind where the center will fall, and try to work out a nice balance of weights and sizes so that the finished bracelet hangs nicely when worn.

Use jump rings and round-nose pliers to attach each charm by opening out the rings ever so slightly, just enough to get them around the charm and the bracelet, and then closing them again to secure. You may need to add an extra jump ring to some of them to get a nice balance and ensure that they all hang the right way.

Don't you think this would be a sweet present? Put together a collection of charms specifically selected with a friend's interests and favorite colors in mind!

*Try adding a pocket in a <u>contrasting fabric</u> **to a blouse of any shape***

diy clothing

There are few things I enjoy as much as shopping in secondhand clothing stores. Finding something preloved, unique, and interesting is thrilling! It's a dream when you find an item that's just about perfect as it is, but some pieces might need the slightest makeover to turn them into something fabulous.

✕ Try adding a pocket in a contrasting fabric to a blouse of any shape. You can also replace or add buttons to freshen up the overall look.

✕ Turn a plain skirt into a fun party skirt by drawing or painting a pattern onto the garment. You could use multisurface paint, fabric paint, or a fabric marker. Be sure to test your materials in an unnoticeable location (such as inside the hem or waistband) if you're not confident about the application results.

✕ Winter woollies can become super-fabulous when you sew on some colorful pom-poms. You could also try fabric patches on the elbows: use a zigzag stitch on the sewing machine for this or a blanket stitch if sewing by hand, to stop the edges from fraying.

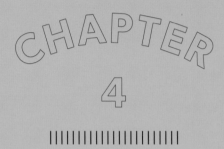

CHAPTER 4

||||||||||||||||||||

COLLECT & RECORD

Memories are made of the little things:
collect and keep small souvenirs
in your journal every day

Record fragments of daily life by collecting everyday items that take your fancy. I collect packaging that's far too pretty to throw away, such as chopstick holders, sugar-stick papers, toothpick holders, wrapping, paper bags, and other everyday items like napkins, flyers, shop cards, coasters, stickers, and tickets.

HINT

Record fragments of <u>daily life</u> **by collecting everyday items**

RECORDING
WITH
*
photos

it's solar powered!

XPAN HASSELBLAD

PINK HOLGA

OLYMPUS TRIP 35

SONY A700

FUJIFILM X20

CANON KISS

Since living in Japan, I've become fascinated with documenting my life through photos. There are few things I enjoy more than strolling around my neighborhood looking for things to photograph. I love seeking hidden details, beautiful light, and special Tokyo moments.

It's addictive sharing pictures on Instagram, and sitting down to retouch images on my computer is another favorite Hello Sandwich pastime. I use Visual Supply Co (VSCO) filters for most of my shots, either on my iMac or iPhone.

When I print out my shots, I use a handful of local photo-printing places. The standard photo size in Japan is smaller than I was accustomed to in Australia, so the novelty aesthetic of printing shots in this size hasn't yet worn off for me.

My photographer Boco-chan introduced me to the most fantastic photography and printing shop in Tokyo called National Photo. The staff are so dedicated, and recently when my favorite uncoated paper manufacturer announced they would discontinue the line, National Photo bought up all the stock that was left because they knew their clients loved it. A local photo store in Shimokitazawa offers a photobook service, turning photos into a gorgeous square-format book on divine paper. Many photo stores around the world offer this service now, and it's such a lovely way to record trips or special events.

With so many options, you can have fun shooting with film and digital cameras, and printing photos as well as simply sharing them online.

handmade camera strap

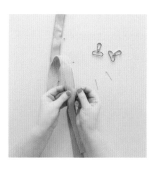

This is a very simple project to keep you looking cute with your camera hanging around your neck, and—best yet—it can be made in less than an hour.

You will need 1¼-inch- (3-cm-) wide sturdy grosgrain ribbon ✕ ¾-inch- (2-cm-) wide contrasting twill ribbon ✕ small piece of leather or faux leather for the tabs ✕ 2 D-rings with clip-on hooks ✕ sewing thread ✕ sewing machine (or hand-sewing equipment) ✕ scissors, pins, needles and general sewing supplies

STEP 1 Measure lengths of grosgrain and twill ribbon so that your camera will hang at a suitable level. Remember that the D-rings and leather tabs will add about 2 inches (5 cm) of length at each end. Here I've used a turquoise grosgrain ribbon and stitched a narrower pink twill ribbon down the center.

STEP 2 Cut two strips of leather (or faux leather) the same width as the wider ribbon and 3¼ inches (8 cm) long.

STEP 3 Pass the leather strip around the flat bar of the D-ring and fold it in half over one end of the ribbon strap. Be sure to tuck the ribbon into the leather by at least ¾ inch (2 cm) so that when the pieces are sewn together, the stitching will hold. Pin in place with sewing pins. Repeat with the other end of the strap.

STEP 4 Stitch a box shape onto the folded leather through all layers. If necessary, add extra stitching to hold the weight of your camera. Some heavier camera bodies or lenses might need a double row of stitching or an X through the middle of the box to keep your special camera safe.

folder file

An accordion folder is a nice way to store collected papers before you place them in a scrapbook or use them in other ways.

You will need sheet of heavy cardstock, painted with gouache ✕ 5 envelopes, all the same size ✕ collage papers ✕ washi tape (such as mt) ✕ string or narrow ribbon ✕ ruler, craft knife, and cutting mat ✕ scissors, glue tape, and craft bond glue ✕ decorative-edge craft punch (optional) ✕ circle craft punch (optional) ✕ metal eyelet and hole punch

STEP 1

STEP 1 Cut a strip from the cardstock the same width as the envelopes plus ¼ inch (5 mm) on each side. The length of the strip should be at least 2½ times the height of the envelopes. If you intend to use a decorative-edge punch, you need to allow approximately ⅜ inch (1 cm) extra for the trim.

STEP 2

STEP 2 Seal each empty envelope using glue tape. Next, stick each of the envelopes together on top of one another: apply a strip of glue tape about ¾ inch (2 cm) inside the outer edges of each envelope. By not gluing right to the edges of the envelopes you will create an accordion effect so the file will expand.

STEP 3

STEP 3 Use a craft knife, ruler, and cutting mat to trim off approximately ⅛ inch (2 to 3 mm) from the top edge of the stack of envelopes. The envelopes should now fold out in a fan when gently pulled open.

STEP 4 Use craft bond glue to attach the outsides of the envelope stack to the cardboard: Lay the cardboard right side down and glue the stack of envelopes with the open top edge facing you, leaving a ¼-inch (5-mm) space around the sides and front edge. Fold the front edge of the cardboard and the envelope stack over and glue the back of the envelope stack to the cardboard. It should now look like a folder.

STEP 4

CONTINUED ON NEXT PAGE . . .

STEP 5

STEP 6

STEP 7

STEP 5 Fold the remaining cardboard over the top of the envelope stack and trim to size if necessary. Decorate the folder with washi tape, collage papers, and stickers.

STEP 6 Now you can use a decorative-edge punch along the edge of the flap. You could also use zigzag or scallop decorative scissors, or cut a scalloped edge freehand.

STEP 7 Use scissors or a circle punch to cut a circle of scrap cardstock (you might want to glue two layers together to make a stronger board). Use a hole punch to punch a hole through the middle of the circle and the center of the flap edge. I always punch these two at the same time so the holes line up. Cut a length of string or narrow ribbon long enough to wrap around the folder file about three times. Thread approximately ¾ inch (2 cm) of it into the hole from the top of the flap. Place the cardboard circle on top of the flap with the punched holes aligned and pop the metal eyelet through the hole, trapping the string in place. Press firmly with the eyelet punch to fix the eyelet.

STEP 8 Finish by wrapping the string once or twice around the folder file and then twisting the loose end around under the cardboard circle. Add a small masking tape flag to the end of the string by folding a piece of masking tape over itself at the end of the string and cutting a small V shape into it. You can also have fun adding beads or little charms to the end of the string for a unique version.

KEEPING

*

a journal

Journaling is one of life's little pleasures. Once you have collected photos, papers, and memories, it's time to collate them.

I always travel with a small craft kit, and if I have downtime on a trip, I work on my journal in my hotel room. Whether you're at home or away, you'll need a nice coffee or drink, some sweet music playing in the background (lullatone.com is a Hello Sandwich favorite), and a free afternoon.

*

JOURNALING &
SCRAPBOOKING

HINT

Divide your journal into specific <u>trips</u>, **events,** **and special moments**

The best thing about scrapbooking is that there are no rules.

collect items you love, like shop cards

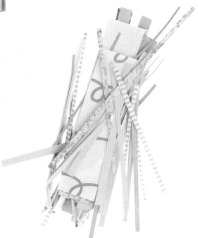

The best thing about journaling and scrapbooking is that there are no rules. There are so many ideas on Pinterest, for example. You can also take a peek at the Hello Sandwich journal board if you need inspiration.

Enjoy making your book layered and textured by including fold-out pages, small envelope pockets, photos, flyers, and other mementos of importance.

You might like to have one book simply for flyers and one book simply for packaging, or you may like to divide your journals into specific trips, events, or special moments.

HANDMADE NOTEBOOKS

When you make your own notebooks, it allows you to customize them exactly the way you like. On these pages you will discover a few tips and suggestions to get you started.

IDEA 1

You could try making an eyelet circle with string to close your book with (see the folder file project on page 96).

IDEA 2

Decorate your books with dot stickers or various other stickers.

IDEA 3

I often use the offcuts from handmade notebooks to make tiny versions. These small notebooks can be great for shopping lists or leaving notes.

IDEA 4

Add masking tape to the spines and corners, not only to make your book more sturdy, but also as a cute design element.

IDEA 5

You can make books any size or shape; with or without covers; stapled, stitched, or bound with string. You can even use an elastic band to hold the pages of your book in place, making it easy to add and subtract pages when necessary.

IDEA 6

Have fun adding labels to the covers of your books.

IDEA 7

If you have bought books that aren't the exact shape or size that you desire, you can always use a craft knife, ruler, and cutting board to trim one book into two, three, or even four smaller books.

*

NOTEBOOK VARIATIONS

1

VARIOUS PAPERS Every page of your handmade notebook needn't be made from the same paper: in fact, it can be quite lovely to have some feature pages inside the book that are a completely different paper stock. You could choose to keep all the pages the same size or you could scatter smaller sheets of paper through the notebook.

feature pages

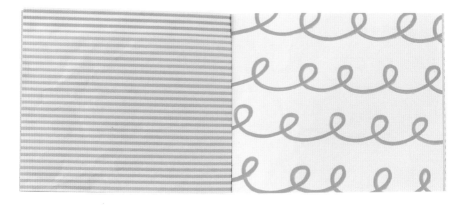

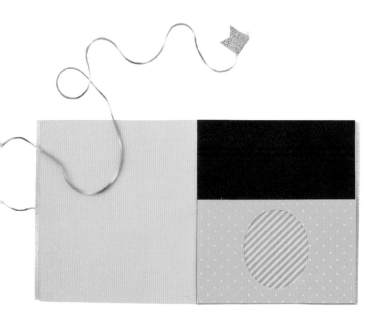

HINT

Glue in little <u>paper bags</u> to **store special treasures**

IDEA
2

ENVELOPE POCKETS Add envelope pockets on the front or back inside covers, or scattered throughout the pages of the book. Make your own pockets by folding over the edges of a piece of paper approximately ⅜ inch (1 cm) on three sides (miter the two bottom corners on a diagonal) and glue the folded edges to a page of the book, or simply glue in an envelope that's open on one edge.

Another way to make little pockets in your notebook is to glue in empty packaging or little paper bags to store special treasures. Once done, you can put little notes, letters, photos, and so on inside.

CUTE
×
PROJECT

osanpo memory book

folded pocket

This little *osanpo* (walking) book was made after a trip to Nishiogikubo with my friend Mami-chan. We met at the station and Mami-chan pulled out a printed Japanese map marked with our walking tour plan. I adored that it was so retro: an actual map, not an app on an iPhone. Mami-chan had mapped out the order in which we should visit each particular craft shop, and we set off for a lovely day together. Along the way I collected shop cards and flyers and took many photos. Back at home I created this little memory book, recording all the special parts of that memorable day. You can make your own book, like I did, or embellish a blank book you already have.

IDEA 1

POCKET BOOK PAGES I made a folded book so each page had a pocket to keep little things like shop cards and so on. You can do this by folding each sheet of paper up at the bottom before binding the book.

IDEA 2

SHOP CARDS I held on to a collection of shop cards so that I can visit them again next time I'm in Nishiogikubo.

IDEA 3

ADD A RETRO MAP

IDEA 4

FIND-A-WORD PUZZLE

I sent a copy of this book to Mami-chan and included a little puzzle with all of the special words from the day hidden in the grid.

pencil case

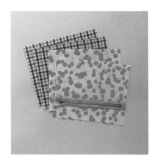

You will need 2 pieces of fabric for the outside ✕ 2 pieces of fabric for the lining ✕ zipper ✕ sewing thread ✕ sewing machine (or hand-sewing equipment) ✕ scissors, pins, needles, and general sewing supplies

STEP 1 Check the length of the zipper and cut the pieces of fabric to the size you'd like the pencil case to be, adding approximately 1-cm (³⁄₈-inch) seam allowance around all sides.

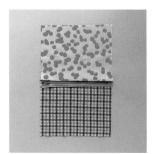

STEP 2

STEP 2 Place one edge of the zipper between one outer piece of fabric and one lining piece, with right sides facing the zipper. Sew along the edge of the zipper through all layers using a straight stitch on a sewing machine or by hand. Repeat this with the remaining pieces of outer and lining fabric on the opposite edge of the zipper.

STEP 3 Lay the pencil case out flat and open the zipper halfway. This is important, or you won't be able to turn it right side out!

STEP 3

STEP 4 Now fold the fabric back so that the two lining pieces are on top of each other (right sides facing) and the two outer pieces are on top of each other (right sides facing) and make sure the zipper is still halfway open. Stitch a ³⁄₈-inch (1-cm) seam around all four edges using a straight stitch, leaving a small gap in the bottom edge of the lining pieces so you can easily turn the pencil case right side out. Once you have sewn around all four edges, cut diagonally across the corners to miter them so they are nice and neat. Turn the pencil case right side out through the gap in the seam and the open zipper. Stitch the gap in the lining closed.

STEP 4

HINT
If you don't have a sewing machine **you can easily stitch this by hand**

*

ZINES

·················

Zines are a brilliant way to record and share your ideas with others. The zines on these pages are made by a few of my friends.

There are no rules when it comes to zine-making: your zine could be a small folded book made from one piece of A4 paper; a handmade, handwritten, and hand-drawn edition of five; or printed in hundreds of copies. The Tokyo Art Book Fair is a wonderful place to get a feel for the range of zines available.

THE WORST FUN by Ebony Bizys and James Goode

I made this zine with my friend James. Over twenty-four hours we documented life. James explains the concept: "Sometimes drifting through time's gentle currents and eddies you're able to watch—as if moving past motorized dioramas in a papier-mâché cave—life actually happening. The collective construction of the present. Minuscule moments of habit. We wanted to mark with a keen eye the details of one day as it's assembled. For twenty-four hours, these were our lives as we lived them."

CATS 'N'. . . by fragola

My friend Mami-chan created this fun package as part of her exhibition in Kyoto in March 2014. The zine includes fun facts about cats, quotes, recommended books, cartoons, music, and so on. It's perfect for people who love cats. The zine came with a stamped wooden spoon, imaginary cat café card, and original music CD.

COUNTING THINGS IN JAPANESE (THINGS I CAN'T COUNT YET) by Grace Lee

This beautiful illustrated zine by my friend Grace is twelve pages to help you learn to count in Japanese. Grace's first zine, it includes drawings on how to count things such as small animals, flat things, and machines and was launched at the Tokyo Art Book Fair.

SPEAK-EASY #13: THE JAPAN ISSUE by Lee Tran Lam

My talented friend Lee Tran Lam describes her zine: "I've been making my zine since 1999. I love what I discover while putting it together: there's a Tokyo bakery that has a nine-year waiting list for its bread, ramen vans exist (and have their own song), and Nestlé's Kit Kat flavors are an edible crash course in Japanese tastes."

Will Reichelt

TEA PARTY BOOK by Sophie et Chocolat

This limited edition zine set was sold at Violet & Claire in 2012. The theme was Tea Party and the pack included a zine, triangular fabric coaster, brooch, handmade tea bag, sticker, and balloon. The zine itself featured ideas and tips on Sophie et Chocolat's favorite party style, favorite tableware, recipes for cookies, and other tea party ideas.

POLKAROS LIFESTYLE by Ros Lee

This zine is a brand book that showcases the philosophy, styles, and concepts behind my friend Ros Lee's lifestyle brand, Polkaros. It takes a look at ideas and realizations, handcrafted works and products produced for the mass market. It's packaged with a customizable tote bag to give readers a taste of the Polkaros handmade culture.

HELLO SANDWICH
zines and blog

HELLO SANDWICH BLOG When I started my blog in 2009, I didn't imagine it would evolve the way it has. One thing to keep in mind when starting a blog is to keep it as broad as possible so you have flexibility to change the style and the content of the blog as your life changes. Be honest, and write in your own style. People love to see shots of daily life. I've never done a regular column on a particular day, but this works for some. In the days of social media, when people are able to get information almost instantly, I think it's important to offer something different on your blog.

I started *Hello Sandwich* as a place to record the things that inspired me. I remember sitting at my little desk in Sydney one night designing my blog's header and signing up with Blogspot. Had I known then what I know now, I think I would have put a lot more effort into designing an actual logo. Without so much as a spellcheck, I hit the Post button on my first blog article and sat back, waiting to see who would actually visit the site.

It was so exciting watching the statistics of *Hello Sandwich* grow over time: seeing visitors from all over the world, then repeat visitors, and then the comments started coming in. I'd soon established a community of readers and commenters and I couldn't wait to get home from work to publish a new post.

Hello Sandwich began as a design and lifestyle blog, but as time went on, it became more personal. When I moved to Tokyo in June 2010, I documented the process, from finding an apartment to my first day living in Tokyo. Those posts are still some of the most commented on. It was surprising to me that people were interested in my ordinary, everyday life.

The ways *Hello Sandwich* has expanded into opportunities for me, and the incredible humans I've connected with, have been life changing.

116

Hello Sandwich's first zine!

HELLO SANDWICH TOKYO GUIDE This was my first-ever zine. It was a collection of my favorite shops and cafés discovered while visiting Tokyo, aimed at first-time visitors to the city.

After living in Japan for a few years, I released an updated version that reviews my favorite Tokyo suburbs, including Shimokitazawa, Harajuku, Shibuya, Nakameguro, Daikanyama, Kichijoji, Shinjuku, and some cool up-and-coming suburbs. While my previous Tokyo guide is a review of the places I loved to visit while vacationing in Tokyo, the updated guide is a peek into all the amazing places I've discovered since moving to Tokyo in 2010.

The *Hello Sandwich Tokyo Guide* is for people who like traveling like a local and visiting hidden places off the beaten path. There are tips on where to rent a bike, the best bike paths, the best coffee, the best craft suppliers, the coolest shops, the cheapest drinks, the most delicious pizza, the best *izakaya* (taverns), the cutest cafés, the best rooftop bar, the coolest hotels (and the cheap and cheerful hotels), the loveliest parks, and even details of a girl who rides a courier bike to a local park to sell her home-baked goods. It's a list of all the places I frequent, making it a local insider's guide to Tokyo.

Also included in the *Hello Sandwich Tokyo Guide* are language essentials and travel tips. In some ways, it's a blogger's guide to Tokyo, and if you'd like to visit the places you've seen on *Hello Sandwich*, then this guide is the zine for you.

HELLO SANDWICH GIFT WRAPPING ZINE

This little zine is sixty-four pages filled with wrapping inspiration and how-to guides to make any present you give look super-cute.

CORRESPONDENCE

*Cute ways to make letter
writing even more fun*

Isn't it so lovely to receive a beautiful handwritten note in your mailbox? The tactile nature of the paper stock; the stamp design; imagining the writer sitting down and penning the note: it's what happiness is made of. One of my favorite pastimes is sitting down and catching up on correspondence. Shown here are a few of the gorgeous letters I've received over the past few years since living in Tokyo.

*

FIRST
THINGS FIRST

It's essential to set yourself up with some beautiful stationery items to make your relaxing letter-writing time more enjoyable. On the following pages are a few Hello Sandwich favorites.

STICKERS Australian brand Blank Goods has a wonderful collection of stickers in all sorts of shapes and sizes to bring fun to your crafts and stationery. Hello Sandwich favorites include fluorescent-pink hearts, mini polka dots, and jumbo circles.

IDEA

2

ERASERS There is just something about a retro pencil eraser that brings some fun to your everyday office supplies. Keep a bunch handy on your desk, even if only for show.

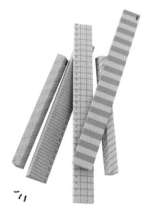

IDEA

3

RULERS These gorgeous wooden rulers are sure to make any measurement-taking fun! Danish design house HAY are the masterminds behind these rulers, which are available from Present & Correct.

IDEA

4

BEAUTIFUL NOTEBOOKS Keep a collection of good-looking notebooks on hand. Trips to Japanese department stores, such as Loft and Tokyu Hands, as well as boutique stationery stores, are habit-forming. Look out for unique cover designs such as polka dots, checks, or a particularly handsome font, then use the notebooks to collect special memories from your life.

My friend David handwrites his blog entries and scans the pages to upload onto his blog. What a lovely idea! Write letters to your friends, then scan the pages and post them electronically. It's almost as good as the real thing.

HINT

These pencils make a <u>lovely gift</u> **for a friend**

HELLO SANDWICH!

♡
♡

IDEA
5

PERSONALIZED PENCILS There's nothing like pencils with your name on them to make you feel like you've made it in the world. I can still remember my Aunty Kerry giving me some personalized "Ebony Bizys" colored pencils as a child. I adore those pencils to this day.

CUTE × PROJECT

Personalize your correspondence by making your own envelopes. It's a fun and simple way to set the mood for when the recipient opens their mailbox to find this handmade surprise. Plus, you'll never have to spend money on envelopes again!

CUTE ✕ PROJECT

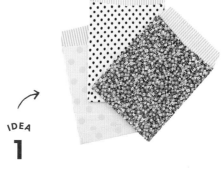

IDEA

1

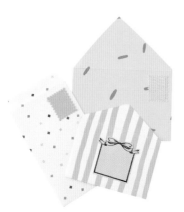

FABRIC-COVERED ENVELOPES Cover paper with pretty fabric before folding to make an unexpected envelope. Use spray adhesive to stick fabric to the envelope base, then use craft bond glue to hold the flaps in place. Line the envelope with tracing paper or patterned waxed paper.

IDEA

2

MINI ENVELOPES These come in handy when you need to give someone something teeny, such as money or tickets. It's also a great way to use up small pieces of cute paper. Adding a mock stamp is a fun way to play with scale, don't you think?

IDEA

3

WINDOW ENVELOPES Here's an envelope that lets you sneak a peek: Cut out a window shape with scissors or a craft knife. I also like to use a Martha Stewart Crafts All Over The Page Punch. Apply transparent paper to the back of the window using glue tape around the edges.

IDEA

4

ENVELOPE TEMPLATES I like to keep a stash of envelope templates on hand; however, if you don't have an envelope template, you can easily make one from an existing envelope. Gently open up the glued edges, being careful not to damage the paper. *Et voilà*, your very own envelope template! Trace this opened-out envelope onto card stock to create a template built to last the crafter's mile!

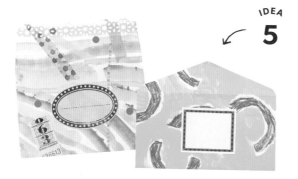

IDEA
5

HAND-PAINTED ENVELOPES Have you ever finished painting and been left with excess paint on your palette? If I find myself in this situation I like to paint pieces of paper in simple patterns, such as stripes, dots, or freestyle designs, to create decorative paper that can be used later for various craft purposes, such as original handmade envelopes.

HINT

Paint decorative designs to make <u>unique</u> **paper envelopes**

IDEA
7

TRANSPARENT ENVELOPES Experiment with various transparent papers such as kitchen waxed paper, tracing paper, tissue paper, and translucent contact paper (with the sticky sides sealed together). If the paper is slightly creased, I like to scrunch it and smooth it out two or three times to enhance the textured effect. Use POSCA pens or other markers to add color. Some waxed papers can be pesky with glue, so craft bond glue might be your best bet. Colorful washi tape along the joins can add security and a nice design effect.

IDEA
6

EYELET CIRCLE-CLOSURE ENVELOPES Use an eyelet punch and a circle of cardboard to create a unique closure for your envelope.

POSTAGE STAMPS In case there weren't already enough reasons for me to adore living in Japan, the stamps here are incredibly good looking. (Hello Kitty stamps, anyone?) These days—as in Australia and all over the world, I imagine—it's common in Japan for the post office to issue a printed label to stick onto your letter in place of a stamp. I'm always curious to read these when I receive letters and notice the issuing post office and so on, but—let's face it—nothing beats actual stamps.

When arranging stamps on an envelope, I enjoy taking time to select different stamp denominations and particular stamps that will look good next to each other on the envelope or package. Rather than lining them up in a neat box or line, I try to arrange them in an organic way, using space in between to create a pretty, mismatched cluster.

In my opinion, the more stamps, the merrier. Mama-Sando caught on to my love of stamps and once sent me an envelope full of Australian fish stamps. There were so many of them that the stamps had to flow over to the back of the envelope. Love you, Mama-Sando!

When I first moved to Tokyo, I quickly made friends with my local post office lady. Once, while I was filling out forms at the counter, she drew a little cartoon version of me on a small piece of paper about the size of a stamp. When I had sent off my packages, she presented me with the drawing as a gift. So gorgeous!

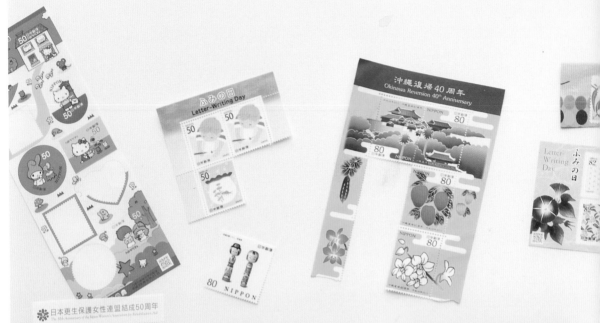

Ebony Bizys. Hello Sandwich
Setagaya-ku 155-0031
Tokyo Japan

thanks ♡
Mom!

Greetings:Autumn
(ぱすくまの1日)

Greetings:Spring

COLLECTING STAMPS Ever since I can recall, I've adored stamps, waiting for the new-release stamps and collecting different kinds. When I was a child, you could buy packets of used stamps. Those were the absolute best! My favorites from those packs were the ones cut straight from an envelope, sometimes including snippets of handwriting or a postmark. Such treasures!

ふみの日
Letter-Writing Day

"Omotenashi" (Hospitality) Flowers Series No. 1

おもてなしの花

シリーズ第一集

SANRIO CHARACTERS
Hello Kitty My Melody
POMPOMPURIN

mini notes

Nothing says *kawaii* (cute) better than a miniature.
Mini letters, mini books . . . you get the idea. If you
just have a tiny something to say, that doesn't mean
that you have to pop it on a sticky note. Make even the
smallest of notes or memos cute with these ideas.

IDEA 1

MINI BOOK Fold a small piece of paper
or lightweight card stock in half, stick
some washi tape to the "spine," mark off
the corners with triangles of tape, and
add a little label in a contrasting color.
Decorate with dots if you're a polka-dot
fan like me. Write a note inside, and
even draw in some dotted lines.

IDEA 2

BOW-SHAPED MINI NOTE
Send a little bow to your friend!
Cut a bow shape out of paper
or lightweight card stock and,
if you like, apply some dotty
stickers for added cuteness.
You can write your message
on the back of the little bow.

IDEA 3

FRAMED NOTE Make your own mini
frames for tiny notes using masking
tape, frame-shaped craft punches,
frame stickers, or rubber stamps.

IDEA 4

LABEL NOTES Use labels or adhesive name tags to convey a short message.

IDEA 5

LITTLE HOUSE A triangle, a rectangle and a window have never looked so cute! Glue these shapes together to make a little house-shaped note for your next tiny correspondence.

IDEA 6

FOLDED NOTE Wrap a tiny note in a piece of paper, adding additional pieces of note paper as required.

IDEA 7

MINI CORRESPONDENCE Create the effect of an airmail envelope by putting striped washi tape around the edges of a small postcard-shaped piece of card stock. Take it to the next level with stamps and an "airmail" or "fragile" sticker. Another idea is to fold a small strip of paper into a mini envelope, trim the flap into a V shape, and seal it with a heart or other sticker of your choice.

collage poster letter

collage
items

LOVE
EBONY

When we send conventional letters—folded pages in an envelope—there is a chance that the recipient may just read the letter once and place it straight back into the envelope. But wouldn't it be nice if the letter took the form of something easily displayed? This collage letter can be displayed on the recipient's wall for days to come. Isn't that so sweet?

You will need   kitchen waxed paper or paper of your choice, about A3 size (11¾ by 16½ inches) **×** stickers, stamps, and collage paper **×** washi tape (such as mt) **×** glue tape **×** bone folder (optional) **×** scissors or craft knife and cutting mat **×** pencil and ruler **×** envelope

STEP 1 I've used kitchen waxed paper for a transparent effect but you could really make this from any paper your heart desires. Once you have cut a piece of paper to the size of your choice, fold it in half over and over again until it fits into the envelope you would like to send it in. There are no rules here.

STEP 2 Now that you have the folds in place, you can open the paper out again and add collage items, such as paper, stickers, masking tape, paper lace or cutouts, and tickets, to each box. In some of the boxes you might like to write notes, while others might contain purely aesthetic elements. It's up to you: enjoy making your own little collage poster letter.

pocket card

Take the traditional greeting card one step further.

You will need lightweight card stock × envelope for mailing × envelopes or paper for the pockets × stickers, stamps, labels and collage paper × washi tape (such as mt) × string, circle punch, eyelet, and hole punch (optional) × glue tape × bone folder (optional) × scissors or craft knife and cutting mat × pencil and ruler

STEP 1 Cut a piece of lightweight card stock to a size that will fit inside your envelope when folded. Score the center with a bone folder or the back of a pair of scissors and fold the card in half.

STEP 2 Add a pocket to each side of the inside of your card. You can use smaller envelopes, or make your own pocket by folding three sides of a piece of paper in 1 cm (⅜ inch) and trimming the bottom two corners on a diagonal to miter them. Apply glue tape to the folded flaps and attach the pocket to the card. Fill these pockets with letters, postcards, photos, mini notes, and so on.

STEP 3 Decorate the inside of the card with stickers, papers, labels, and assorted stamps. Enjoy decorating the front with washi tape and other materials. In this version, I used gold foil letters to spell out the name of my friend, but you could decorate the cover in any way your heart desires. It could be sweet to attach a photo of yourself and your friend on the front. Happy memory making!

STEP 4 Of course you could simply leave the card folded and call it a day, but if time is on your side, why not add a string closure? See page 98 for instructions on making a string closure with a hole punch, eyelet, and string. The string can be as long as you like. A very thin piece of string can wrap around the card two or three times, but if it's a thicker string, once is enough. At the end of the string you can add beads, a tape flag, or a knot to keep the string from fraying. To make a tape flag, place the end of the string in the middle of a 2-inch (5-cm) length of masking tape, fold it over on top of itself, and snip out a V shape.

STEP **1**

STEP **2**

STEP **3**

STEP **4**

original stamps

PHOTO STAMPS

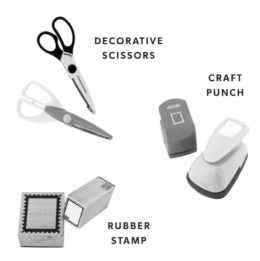

DECORATIVE SCISSORS

CRAFT PUNCH

RUBBER STAMP

PHOTO STAMPS Print some of your favorite photos at postage-stamp size and make them into mock stamps. If you're a whiz with photo-editing software you might like to import your photos and add some fun text, such as the price or your name, or even your country. Once you print these stamps out, cut them out with scissors or pinking shears and add them to your outgoing mail for a personalized and unexpected crafty touch.

CRAFT PUNCH STAMPS Stock up on craft punches that make postage stamp shapes. I have a few different types that I use regularly, some of which also emboss— super cute! Experiment with adding a small rectangle of contrasting paper to each stamp to create a border effect. Or have fun illustrating original designs on each stamp! It's a great way to use up scraps of paper that you might have left over from a craft project. Make a big batch of stamps while you're watching TV.

RUBBER STAMP STAMPS If you're lucky, you might be able to find a postage-stamp rubber stamp. If not, how about carving your own from an eraser? Personalized and handmade always have a certain charm. I've handpainted some white lightweight card stock with fluorescent-pink gouache before stamping the border with black ink; but wouldn't it look super sweet if you stamped floral paper or polka-dot paper? Have fun experimenting with patterns. Use regular scissors or pinking shears to trim the stamped stamps into stamp shapes.

PINKING SHEARS STAMPS If you have pinking shears on hand, you can pretty much make mock stamps from any type of paper. As well as traditional zigzag shears, you can find paper scissors with decorative blades from large and small zigzags to scallops and curves. Try experimenting with different blades and various types of paper.

playful post

MAIL TIP 1

DOLL DELIVERY This *kokeshi* doll appeared in my mailbox one day, and I was sure it had been hand-delivered, but then I noticed the stamp and label: Mami-chan had mailed it from Kyoto to Tokyo! I unscrewed the bottom of the doll to find a scroll letter tightly bound inside the body.

MAIL TIP 2

WATERMELON ENVELOPE This little watermelon letter was sent to me by Mami-chan one summer. It's a super-cute example that shows that mail doesn't have to be a regular size and shape!

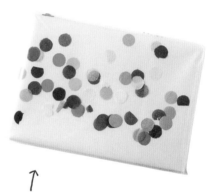

MAIL TIP 3

CELLOPHANE CONFETTI Transform a plain envelope into a fun package by popping it into one hundred percent biodegradable cellophane bag, filling the bag with confetti, and sealing with tape. Write the recipient's address on a label attached to the front of the package so the confetti doesn't cover the address in transit.

MAIL TIP 4

MESSAGE IN A BOTTLE Mami-chan is the master of cute mail. Once I received this teeniest of bottles with a tiny scroll letter. Smaller than a ¥100 coin! I couldn't wipe the smile off my face the entire time I was opening this incredible package and reading the scrolled note!

MAIL TIP 5

SWEETS BOX PACKAGE After a crafternoon at my friend Kazumi-chan's house, I received a little box in the mail. It was filled with paper cupcake liners full of the elastics and ribbons that we had used that day. Sweet! I had never seen such a cute little postage box before.

mailed from a retro postbox!

MAIL TIP 6

FAN MAIL When Mami-chan went on a trip within Japan, she mailed me this amazing wooden fan postcard. After I had received this letter she sent me a photo of herself mailing it from an amazing retro Japanese mailbox: what a special treat!

garland letter

....

STEP 1

A lovely way to ensure that your friend or loved one gets as much enjoyment from your letter as possible is to create something garland-like that can be displayed in their home. Think party garland, but on a smaller scale. Collect some special pieces of paper that you love and that work well together in combination, and cut them into similar-size shapes, such as tags or triangles. You might also like to cut collage pieces from a magazine or secondhand book.

Can't
Wait
to
see
you
!

STEP

← **2**

Once you have collected your paper pieces and cut them into your desired shapes, it's time to attach them to a length of string. I've used a fluffy Avril string here, but feel free to use any string, ribbon, or yarn you like. Add the garland letter pieces by folding washi tape to connect each garland piece to the string. Finally, write your message on the back of the garland letter and carefully place it in an envelope or box to mail to your friend.

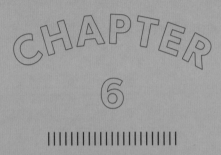

GIFT WRAPPING

*Create fun and colorful original
wrappings using the variety
of materials you have on hand*

CUTE
+
PROJECT

wrapping ideas

Gift giving is such an important part of Japanese culture that it should come as no surprise to learn that there is a lot of attention paid to wrapping gifts beautifully. Bookstore shelves are full of wrapping tutorials and almost every shop offers a gift-wrapping service. Spend some time here and you'll soon find yourself involved with this special ritual. More often than not, I've planned the wrapping before I've even bought the gift.

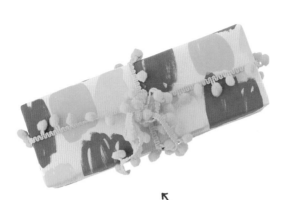

HAVE FUN!!

IDEA
1

POSCA AND POM-POMS Take a plain piece of paper and use a POSCA paint marker (or marker of your choice) to draw a design onto the paper. Try not to agonize over making the drawing too neat or perfect, as you'll only see sections of the paper once your gift is wrapped. If you find that you create a piece of paper that you absolutely adore, why not scan, photograph, or photocopy it before you wrap the present? This will give you the option to reuse the design (even if only as a base) in the future. Finish off with some pom-pom braid.

IDEA
2

STICKERS Anyone who knows me will know that my go-to technique for wrapping is to cover the paper with little stickers. Usually I use small dot stickers, but you can also use metallic stickers, such as little gold hearts. Using stickers to decorate a present is one of the quickest and simplest ways to add a sense of fun to your gift-wrapping style.

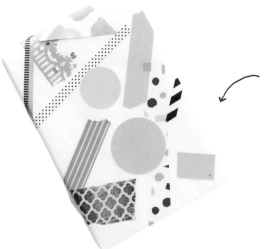

IDEA

3

COLLAGE PAPER Cover a plain piece of wrapping paper with a collage of small pieces of masking tape, paper, and even some craft-punch shapes. You can use the original piece of paper to wrap the present, or photocopy it if you would like to use the design over and over again.

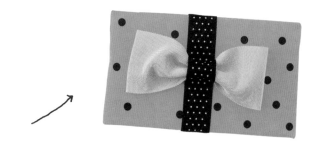

IDEA

4

RIBBON Use wide ribbon to create a bow for your present by folding the ends to the middle to make a loop, with the ends just overlapping. Stitch through all layers in the center of the loop and pull the stitches tight to gather the ribbon into a bow shape. Wrap a small loop of contrasting ribbon around the center. Attach your bow to the present by hand-stitching or using glue.

HINT *My go-to technique* <u>for wrapping</u> **is adding lots of little stickers**

IDEA

5

BELT Jazz up your present by adding a small strip of contrasting paper as a belt. If you have a craft edge punch you may like to punch along the edges of this strip for a fun effect. Fold a thin strip of washi-tape-covered lightweight cardboard to form a little bow, and finish off with a gemstone sticker in the center.

IDEA

6

CREPE-PAPER BOW A simple and quick way to add a handmade element to gift wrapping is to make a crepe-paper bow. Cut a rectangle of crepe paper no larger than your present box. Next, squeeze the crepe paper in the middle, forming a bow shape, and fasten with some string. Attach the crepe-paper bow to the present with some cute string, ribbon, or twine.

HINT

Make it dazzling with a gemstone **sticker in the center**

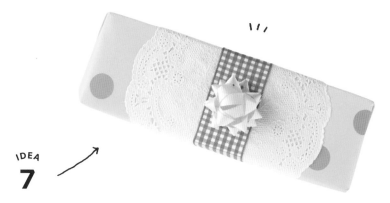

IDEA

7

DOILY The simplest style of wrapping can be transformed easily by adding a paper doily. Try experimenting with gold, silver, and pastel-colored paper doilies. You could also spray-paint plain white paper doilies to create a unique effect. Hold the doily in place with some tape glue and fasten with a ribbon of your choice.

Photocopy or scan your designs to reuse them!

IDEA

8

WASHI PAPER Simply stick some torn pieces of washi tape over a piece of plain-colored wrapping paper to create an original design. Add a metallic ribbon or a present topper of your choice to finish the look.

CUTE
×
PROJECT

cellophane bags

....

Cellophane bags are a quick, simple, and cute way to wrap a small gift. Natural cellophane is one hundred percent biodegradable, too! Here are three unique ways to use these bags.

MINI HANDBAG Pop some colorful shredded paper into the bag, and then place a small gift on top of this cushion of paper. Next, lay some string or ribbon across the top of the bag, just above the filling. Double fold the top of the bag over the string and seal with a sticker or tape. Tie the string at the top in a bow to form a little handle.

HINT

Finish off by adding <u>dot stickers</u> **all over the bag**

MONEY BAG You can put all sorts of things into a cellophane bag: confetti, shredded paper, beads, sequins, tinsel. For this bag, I sandwiched tinsel and paper between clear contact paper. Using this technique you are able to create the effect of confetti inside the bag, without the mess. Enclose the goodies with some string and a charm. Finish with dot stickers.

FLAT PACK This type of wrapping is great for flattish gifts. Cut a piece of cardboard slightly smaller than the bag and place it behind the gift inside the bag. Cut another piece of cardboard the width of the bag and fold it in half over the top of the bag. Secure it with glue tape or staples. Use a craft punch with a decorative edge for extra cuteness.

handmade paper bag

STEP
1

You will need wrapping paper ✖ wide washi tape (such as mt) ✖ handles from an old paper bag (see step 4) ✖ collage materials (optional) ✖ glue tape ✖ craft bond glue ✖ bone folder (optional) ✖ scissors

STEP 1 You can make your own paper bag from most types of paper: I've used pink floral wrapping paper here. Cut a rectangle twice as wide as you want the finished bag to be and about 4 inches (10 cm) taller. Turn the paper over so the patterned side is facing down. Fold 2 inches (5 cm) over at the top edge and smooth the crease with a bone folder. Use glue tape and washi tape to secure this fold in place.

STEP
2

STEP 2 Fold both side edges to the center so that they meet with a small overlap of approximately ⅜ inch (1 cm). Secure these edges together with washi tape, or for a more simple look you could use glue tape. Make a crease for the base of the bag, about the same width as the size you would like the base of the bag to be. Approximately 2 to 2½ inches (5 to 6 cm) is a good size.

STEP 3 Open the top layer of the base toward you and press the corners into a triangle shape as shown in the photo.

STEP
3

STEP 4 Fold up the bottom edge of the base to meet the fold above it. Then, fold the top edge of the base down to the same fold and tape the edges together with wide mt tape. Now, cut some handles from an existing shopping bag and attach them to the inside top of the bag with craft bond glue. Press firmly to hold in place. If needed, secure the handles in place with some washi tape for extra support. You could also experiment with string, pipe cleaners, or ribbons as alternative handles. Decorate the bag with a collage of paper and fabric, if you like.

STEP
4

CUTE
×
PROJECT

present toppers

IDEA
1

ORIGAMI BOWS The art of folding paper is a very Japanese skill that turns simple squares of paper into complex decorative forms. Pop online for video tutorials on how to make cute bows like this, find some origami paper, and start playing.

IDEA
2

RIBBON ROSETTE Fold a length of ribbon zigzag style so there are at least two bends and a tail on each side. Use a hairpin to temporarily hold the ribbon folds in the center, then use a sewing needle and thread to stitch through all the layers in the center, gently pulling the bends and tails into a nice rounded shape as you go. Finish by trimming a V-shaped notch into the two ribbon ends.

HINT *Try your hand at* <u>origami</u> **for a true Japanese bow**

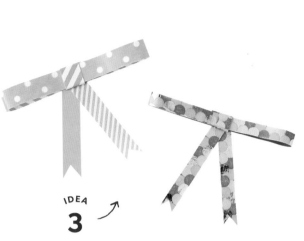

SIMPLE BOW This might be the easiest bow on earth. Simply take a rectangle of paper, fabric, crepe paper, or even a pretty plastic bag, and form it into a bow shape by scrunching it in the middle and fastening with string. You could use pinking shears to make a zigzag edge. Why not sew a pom-pom or button into the center of the bow? Have fun!

WASHI TAPE RIBBON You can make these bows in any size you like. To start, stick some washi tape of your choice in a long strip onto some paper or lightweight card stock. Turn the paper over and stick more tape in the same spot on the reverse side of the paper. Repeat the process so that you have two double-sided strips. Now using a craft knife and ruler, trim the paper into two strips approximately the width of the tape. You might need to trim them slightly skinnier to ensure the lightweight stock is completely covered. Now fold the ends of one of the strips to the center and secure them in place by wrapping some tape around the center of your bow. From the other strip of tape-covered card, cut two tails, and attach them to the back of the bow using craft bond glue. Sometimes I use a combination of glue tape and then craft bond glue. The glue tape helps hold the pieces in place long enough for the craft bond glue to dry, making a very secure bond. Trim a small V-shaped notch into the end of each tail.

PAPER ROSETTES These little rosettes are a great way to use up odd bits of paper. I've used a Martha Stewart Crafts Scalloped Circle Layering Punch, which makes these pretty little scalloped-edge circles, but you could use scissors to cut a circle, a star, or even a little heart. Embellish with stickers, spangles, and gemstones, and finish with two strips of lightweight card stock to make the tails. Because these rosettes are flat, you can use them to decorate letters and envelopes as well as presents.

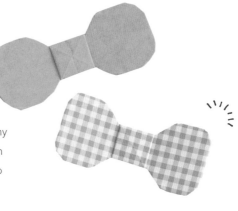

ROUND ORIGAMI BOW Use one of the many tutorials online to make an origami bow, then round the corners off by folding the points to the inside or trimming them with scissors.

BENTO PATTY TOPPER Another little quick and cheerful present topper idea is to layer various sizes of bento patties (or paper cupcake liners) inside one another. I've added a fabric flower and a sequin to this topper but you could add anything your little heart desires. Use craft bond glue to fasten each layer together, or push a split pin through to secure the whole arrangement. It would be so cute with gold or silver foil cupcake liners, don't you think?

SIMPLE ROSETTE Fold a length of ribbon with a half twist so that the right sides are facing up, then cross them over and fasten with a staple. Next, glue a circle of lightweight card stock over the staple (you can either cut a circle with scissors or use a circle punch). To finish, add spangles or decorative stickers to the circle shape and voilà—the rosette is ready!

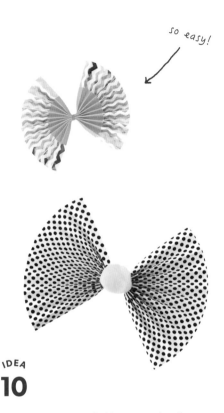

so easy!

IDEA
9

WASHI POM-POM This little pom-pom is a great way to recycle plastic bags. Cut six pieces of plastic bag approximately 3½ x 5½ inches (9 x 14 cm). If you fold the bag neatly, you can cut all the layers at once. Add some washi tape strips along the two long edges on each piece. Now layer all six pieces on top of one another and accordion fold all the layers together, with the tape on the outsides, at once. While it's still folded, trim the taped ends into rounded shapes and fasten the folds in the center with some string. Now it's time to open out each layer and see your washi tape pom-pom take shape! Note: If you have a plastic bag that already has a nice color or pattern, you might not need to use washi tape at all, as it may already be cute enough! Another tip is to try layering different colored plastic bags on top of each other to make a multicolored pom-pom.

IDEA
10

ACCORDION BOW Fold a rectangle of paper or lightweight card stock accordion style. Try to keep the folds as narrow as you can so the bow is nice and flat: approximately ¼ to ⅜ inch (5 to 10 mm) is a good guideline. Tie the center of the paper bow with a piece of string and fan out the edges. Use craft bond glue to add a pom-pom to the center of the bow.

CUTE + PROJECT

ribbon rosette

You will need 3 yards (2.5 m) of 1-inch- (2.5-cm-) wide ribbon × button, pom-pom, or embellishment for the center × short lengths of ribbon for the back tails × small piece of felt × scissors, sewing thread, and needle × craft bond glue (optional)

STEP 1 Start off the rosette by folding ¼ inch (5 mm) under the end of the ribbon and secure it in place with a needle and a knot of sewing thread. Carefully fold the ribbon into neat pleats, making a small stitch at the base of each pleat to keep them in place.

STEP

2

STEP 2 Curve the pleats as you go, keeping the center hole as small as possible.

STEP 3 Once you have finished the full circle of pleats, trim off any excess ribbon and finish by stitching the end of the ribbon to the first fold at the back of the rosette.

STEP 4 Now it's time to sew or glue your button, pom-pom, or other embellishment into the center of the pleated ribbon rosette. Sew some lengths of different patterned ribbons to the back of the rosette to make the tails. Finally, cover the back of the rosette with a circle of felt. If you like, attach a brooch pin to the back of the rosette so the receiver can wear it as a corsage or pin it to their tote bag once they have opened the gift!

STEP

3

HINT

Add a brooch pin so your friend can <u>wear it</u> **right away!**

STEP

4

CUTE × PROJECT

gift tags

One of the simplest ways to create a handmade effect with gift wrapping is to make your own gift tags. You can sit down and make a big batch in one "crafternoon" and store them in a little box so they are on hand for those times of need. Make tags in various shapes and sizes so that you've got yourself covered for any size present. It's a fantastic way to use up scraps of paper, card stock, and short lengths of string. An eyelet punch is a great way to attach the string to the tag and give it a polished and professional look.

IDEA 1

BOW TAG A bow tag is easy to create by cutting lightweight cardboard into the shape of a bow and adding either a heart-shape piece or a disk of lightweight card stock in the center. Finish with a piece of narrow ribbon attached with an eyelet punch.

IDEA 2

CIRCLE TAGS It's time to take out your circle punch and get punching! If you don't have a circle punch you can trace around a glass and use scissors to cut around the shape. Circle-shaped tags look cute just as they are, but you can take your tags to the next level in a few different ways. Use glue to attach another circle of heavy cardstock approximately ⅜ inch (1 cm) larger to the back of your circle and use fringing scissors to fringe the edges of the cardboard. (You can also use regular scissors to cut a fringe, it just takes a little longer.) Another favorite trick is to embellish your circle gift tag with some gemstone stickers.

IDEA 3

BOOKMARK STYLE A long and slim gift tag can easily be reused as a cute little bookmark. Add some washi tape to the sides of a strip of cardboard and trim off the top two corners to create a mitered corner. Each time your friend opens their book, they will remember the gorgeous present you gave them and smile.

a favorite

IDEA

5

WASHI TAPE TAGS A quick and colorful way to create an original gift tag is to apply torn pieces of different colored washi tape to a tag.

IDEA

4

CONTACT TAGS This is a Hello Sandwich favorite. I find it almost impossible to throw out tiny scraps of paper or leftover punched papers. I have a small tray on my desk where I keep all these goodies. Sandwich these precious pieces of paper between sheets of self-adhesive clear contact paper. Next, use a ruler and craft knife to cut the contact paper into the shape of a gift tag. Finish by making a hole for some string at the top of the tag with an eyelet punch (or regular hole punch). Finally, glue a small piece of paper onto the front so that you can easily write your message on the tag. Alternatively, write your message on paper and press it between the contact paper as well.

IDEA

6

COLLAGE TAGS Have fun assembling complementary pieces of paper to create a collage. Try experimenting with lace paper, tickets, labels, and grid papers. I like to simply place the layers on top of each other without gluing them, and hold them in place only with the eyelet at the top of the tag. Try covering lightweight paper with floral fabric using spray adhesive to bond the two pieces together. Next, add some short lengths of ribbon to the top of the tag before attaching ribbon or string with an eyelet punch.

CUTE × PROJECT

original wrapping paper

IDEA 1

HAND-PAINTED PAPER One of my favorite types of wrapping paper. The options are endless: paint lightweight butchers' paper with gouache paints and glitter glue; create a watercolor effect by blending watered-down gouache paints; make a color-block design; or paint some freehand spots or stripes.

IDEA 2

DIP-DYED PAPER Set up your own little dyeing station by mixing water-based paint with water in a plastic cup. Fold a sheet of washi paper, or other lightweight tissue paper, into folded triangles and fasten with rubber bands. Next, dip the edges of the folded papers into the cups. Wait until the paint has dried before opening the paper out to see your design! It's so much fun to see how it turns out!

IDEA 3

COLLAGE PAPER Decorate a piece of paper Matisse-style by using glue tape to attach small scraps of paper. Or, you could adorn the paper with small torn pieces of washi tape. If your paper is a standard size, you could take it to a printing shop and photocopy the page so you can keep copies to use in the future.

POLKA-DOT PAPER A Hello Sandwich favorite: Apply some dot stickers to a plain piece of paper to create a polka-dot pattern. It's also fun to apply dot stickers to tissue paper. Experiment with various colors and sizes of stickers. These dots are easy to find at local stationery stores and are quick and easy to apply, yet create a fun and impressive impact. Win–win!

SPRAY-PAINTED PAPER

Pop on a little facemask (or tie a handkerchief around your mouth and nose) and have fun spraying some pieces of paper with aerosol paint. Make speckled effects by letting the paint drip out of the can, or blended effects by holding the can at different angles.

HAND-DRAWN PAPER

I've used POSCA paint markers for this handmade wrapping paper, but you could use any markers you have on hand. Experiment with patterns, shapes and colors. For inspiration, you might like to peek at the Hello Sandwich art and patterns on Pinterest. Stripes and polka dots are generally foolproof!

candy necklace wrapping

Everyone loves candies, but this fun gift is more about their playful wearable aspect than just handing over a bag of sweets.

STEP 1

You will need fabric × candies × string × ribbons × charms × tulle and cellophane (optional) × beads and fake flowers (optional) × scissors and pinking shears

STEP 1 Cut squares of fabric slightly bigger than the candies. Be sure to leave enough room to wrap the candy in the fabric and also enough room at each end to tie the wrapper closed.

STEP 2 Roll a candy in fabric and tie the ends with string. Don't trim off the ends of the string yet, as you'll need them later. Repeat this step with each of the candies. If you have any tulle, or perhaps some cellophane, you can also wrap some candies in this.

STEP 2

STEP 3 Arrange all the wrapped candies in a necklace shape on a flat surface and decide which colors will go where to make your necklace layout. Once you have decided the positioning of each candy, it's time to start tying each candy onto another piece of string. The string should be long enough to fit all the candies on it. Simply tie both ends of each candy to the longer piece of string, using the tails of string from the wrapping. If you want to add some beads to the necklace, thread them onto the string as you go. Repeat this technique until you have tied all the candies onto your necklace string.

STEP 3

STEP 4 Next you can add some charms, ribbons, or fake flower decorations to the necklace by simply tying them on. To finish off, tie a length of ribbon (I've used two different types on this necklace) to the ends of the necklace string, and the candy necklace is good to go—yay!

STEP 4

✱ OSUSOWAKE WRAPPING

I love the concept of *osusowake* (sharing). It's a Japanese word that describes one of the most charming Japanese customs: the giving of something inexpensive, but important, between friends. For example, when you buy a roll of stickers or box of candies and find yourself with more than you need, you might share a small section of them with a friend.

In the past I've received an *osusowake* of some mini packets of sixteen-grain rice from a friend. I had previously mentioned that I was looking for quinoa in Tokyo and she had found a rice mix that included quinoa as one of its sixteen grains. My friend is so sweet that she translated the instructions into English and included the packaging should I wish to buy it again when I ran out. It was such a sweet gesture!

Another time, after I went for a crafternoon at my friend Kazumi-chan's house, I tried to make a folder like the one I had made at her house, only to realize I needed the special elastic she had. A day or two later, a sample pack of every color of the elastic and some ribbons arrived in a candy box at my house (see page 143)! They were packaged so prettily inside paper cupcake liners, I almost cried. It was another *osusowake*.

The history of the word *osusowake* is really lovely. It has its origins back when handmaking kimonos was very popular. The leftover fabric from making the kimono was shared with other friends. From what I can gather, *suso* is "hem" and *wakare* is "to share," so it's like the division and sharing of excess fabric. To me, this is so beautiful and poetic.

IDEA
1

TEA These days tea bags often come in such divine packaging. Share the gift of some downtime with your friend by popping two pretty tea bags in a mini pocket card. Add some tie tabs to the edge of your card that will securely keep your *osusowake* in place.

IDEA
2

SMALL CLIPS We all need clips to keep things in order, but rarely do we splurge on this office essential. Treat your friend to some super-cute clips that are bound to make filing and organizing fun! Slip them into a handmade envelope bag: simply trim a sealed envelope with some pinking shears, and attach mini pipe-cleaner handles with washi tape.

IDEA
3

STRAWS Add a little bit of fun to your friend's Friday night drinks by sharing some of your cute straws with them. When they finish work, kick their kitten heels off, and relax, they will happily sip their sparkling drinks with these straws. Pop the straws into a handmade tissue-paper bag with stapled paper edges.

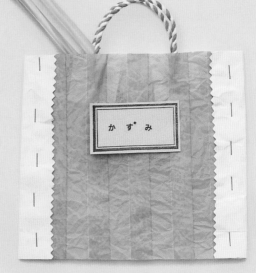

IDEA 4 **RIBBONS** Share some lengths of ribbon with your friends. Even the shortest scraps will come in handy if your friend is the crafty type. Try putting the ribbons into the teeniest paper bag so they peek out when you're passing the gift to your friend. How cute!

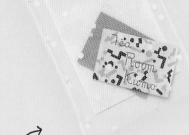

IDEA 5 **FABRIC FLOWERS** Fabric flowers are such a great craft-cupboard essential. They can be used for both paper and fabric crafts. Why not try wrapping some in a mini bouquet as a little *osusowake* for your friend?

IDEA 6 **STICKERS** Stickers often come in packs with multiple sheets. Share the love by giving a sheet or two to your friend in a little hand-sewn tulle bag.

IDEA 7

BEADS AND BUTTONS Share beads and buttons in a little dotty-sticker-covered jar that your friend might be able to reuse in the future. The buttons shown here are fabric-covered ones made using a simple kit. If you can get your hands on one of these kits from your local craft or sewing store I can highly recommend it. It's a great way to use up scraps of fabric and create beautiful original buttons. Finish off the *osusowake* with a handmade collage gift tag tied around the rim of the jar.

IDEA 8

ASSORTED PAPERS Spread the paper love with a friend by making a little assorted paper pack. I have potentially the biggest paper collection in Shimokitazawa, but I still get super-excited when a friend gives me some new paper. There's something inspiring about new paper, much the same as a stack of white printer paper, or a new set of felt-tip pens. So much potential. Snip off pieces of some of your favorite papers and pop them into a transparent envelope to share with your friend. Make your friend a special label if you have time.

PARTIES & EVENTS

*It's the little details that make
your celebrations—big or small—
into happy memories for your
family and friends*

CUTE LIVING TIP
*
DECORATIONS

PASTEL POWER!

Decorating for parties is the best fun, even in the tiny Hello Sandwich HQ. Long before the guests arrive and the food hits the table, I enjoy planning cute tablescapes with my favorite plates and accessories. My mom, Mama-Sando, always does a little sketch of her table before Christmas lunches so she can get an idea of which color and shape of plate will go where. The apple doesn't fall far from the tree, as they say.

balloons

What says "party" better than a bunch of balloons?
For a simple handmade touch, add some stickers to
your balloons. I've used gold dot stickers and some
large fluorescent-pink star stickers from Blank Goods
to create a fun atmosphere. Add some sparkly tassels
to your balloons with the metallic streamers from party
poppers. Fancy taking it to the next level? Try making
your own tassels using crepe paper or tissue paper,
but if you have helium-filled balloons, be sure not to
make the tassels too heavy or the balloon might not
float. If you intend to tie your balloons to hang them,
however, feel free to add as many tassels as your little
heart desires. Confetti System and Geronimo Balloons
are the masterminds behind this balloon-tassel craze.
The gorgeous multicolored tassel on the far right was
created by the amazing Jihan of Geronimo Balloons.

HINT

Feel free to add as many <u>tassels</u> **as your heart desires**

garlands

Garlands are a Hello Sandwich party essential. With
so many different ways to make garlands, and with
their high-impact appearance and ease of storage,
there is practically no excuse for not having a garland
at your next celebration. If you're a whiz on a sewing
machine or you love to hand sew, why not stitch some
of your favorite fabric pieces along a piece of bias tape
or ribbon? If you have a favorite craft punch, why not
punch a stack from heavyweight paper and sew them
into a garland by running them through your sewing
machine? Use ribbons, fabric, or washi tape too.

HINT

× Keep garlands safe and
sound between parties by
folding them either around
a piece of cardboard, or
by folding the pieces on
top of one another, and
then popping them into
an envelope or bag for
safekeeping. Use an elastic
band to hold them together
if need be.

CUTE
+
PROJECT

cute drinks

Add an element of fun and celebration to your drink or food with the perfect straw, skewer, or topper!

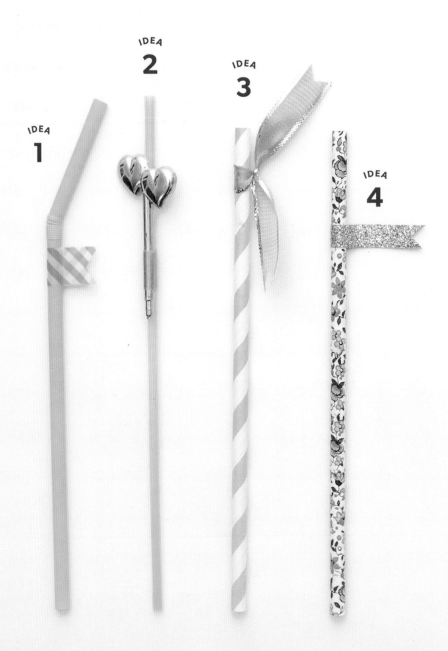

IDEA 1

IDEA 2

IDEA 3

IDEA 4

WASHI TAPE FLAG Fold a piece of washi tape around the straw (leaving enough room for the person to drink) and trim a little V shape into the tape.

CHARM Use washi tape to attach a small charm near the top of a straw.

RIBBON Tie a short length of ribbon near the top of a straw. Trim the ends of the ribbon into a V shape.

GLITTER TAPE Fold over a piece of metallic glitter tape near the top of your straw and trim the end into a V shape. This tape is from Blank Goods.

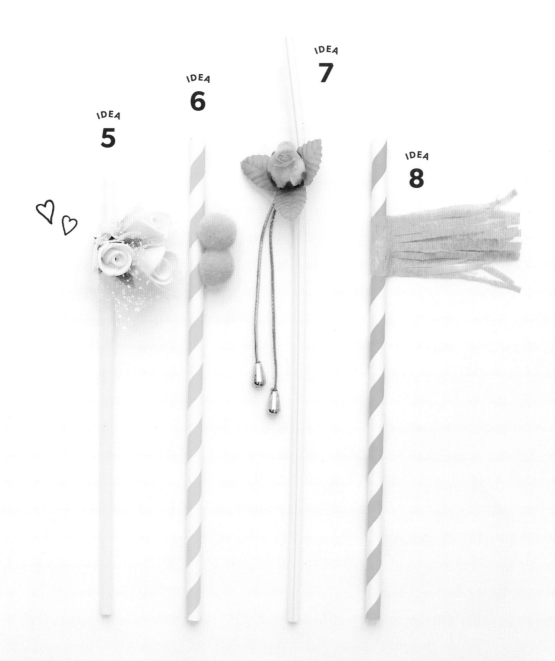

IDEA 5

IDEA 6

IDEA 7

IDEA 8

WIRE FLOWER If you can find fake flowers on wire, just twist them around near the top of a straw. If you can't find such a product, thread florists' wire through some fake flowers.

POM-POM Use craft bond glue to attach two pom-poms to the side of a straw, near the top.

FLOWER STRING Attach a little flower tie or a brand-new floral hair tie near the top of a straw.

CREPE-PAPER FRINGE Use tape glue to secure a length of crepe paper, folded over near the top of a straw. Use fringing or regular scissors to create a fringe.

party ice

PARTY TIP 1

Add some herbs or edible flowers to the next batch of ice cubes you make so that your party guests can enjoy a pretty floral element in their drink. Be sure to use a large silicone ice tray, because larger ice cubes melt more slowly. To get the clearest ice cubes, use distilled water that has been boiled and cooled before use. Always use edible flowers and herbs that have not been treated with toxic chemicals. Work in layers to suspend the flowers in the cubes. To layer, place the flowers face down in the bottom of the ice tray and fill it about a third of the way to the top with water. Freeze until solid and repeat until the tray is full and completely frozen.

CUTE LIVING TIP

*

TABLE
DECORATION

SHARE WITH FRIENDS

HINTS

✗ Good quality crystal glasses and bubbly drinks are a great way to get a party off to a good start.

✗ A dark-colored tablecloth helps set the tone for a fun and relaxed mood. If anything is spilled on the cloth, stains are easy to cover and remove.

✗ Fresh flowers, even just a small bunch, add life and color to a party table.

✗ Linen napkins are a must. A mixed set can be even more lovely than a matching set! Make your own napkin holders with flowers on a piece of florists' wire.

✗ Handmade place tags are a gorgeous addition to any table.

✗ Keep food and plates colorful when setting the dishes on the table. Choose plates that complement the dishes.

When you're deciding on a party menu, choose food that's easy to eat while enjoying the company of friends. Foods that can be eaten with one hand while holding the plate with the other are great if your guests won't be sitting at a table to eat. Avoid drippy sauces and food that must be eaten hot.

party hats

Having a few handmade party hats on standby helps to get friends into a festive vibe and enjoy a few laughs. You can embellish existing party hats or make your own. Add trims such as tinsel, pom-poms, flowers, ribbons, sequins, and stickers for an original party-hat collection.

IDEA
1

photo-booth decoration

Streamers and painted backdrops not only look great as decorations, but are a great location for guests to pose for photo-booth-style pictures during the event.

IDEA 1: STREAMER WALL Take a length of dowel or a curtain rod and attach lengths of colored streamers. Simply fold a streamer over the rod and use masking tape to attach the end of the streamer at the back of the rod. Feel free to add some metallic streamers if that's your thing. Once you're happy with the arrangement of the streamers, it's time to hang your streamer backdrop on the wall.

IDEA 2: WASHI TAPE BACKDROP You can either apply washi tape directly to your wall or to a very large piece of cardboard, foam core board, or lightweight wooden board. I've used foam core and mt-brand CASA tape (wide washi tape for interiors) for this backdrop. If you can't get your hands on this mt tape, you could use any type of decorative tape, or you could also hand-paint the stripes on the backdrop.

IDEA 3: MATISSE-INSPIRED COLLAGE Take some colorful scraps of paper or a pack of origami paper, and randomly cut the pieces into shapes of your choice. Arrange these pieces on a colored background (I've used black but of course you could use any color your heart desires), and glue them down at the very last stage.

*
PARTY PIECES

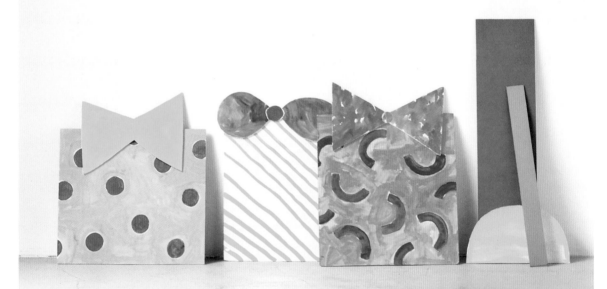

PARTY TIP 3

GIANT PRESENTS Paint some giant presents directly onto foam core board. These pieces look cute just sitting around your event space, and will double as wonderful photo booth props. The sturdy nature of the foam core will allow you to reuse these props at future events, ensuring all your hard work pays off.

PARTY TIP 4

CONFETTI FLOOR Sure, it's hard to clean up, but everyone loves a confetti floor. Go on, sprinkle a package on the floor, just this once! If you've made the decision to go with it, why not get the camera ready for a "confetti sprinkling" event and capture some amazing moments with confetti in midair?

PARTY-IN-A-BOX

Friends who might not be able to attend shouldn't miss out on all the fun. Pack up a box and be sure to include a party hat, garland, candy, Champagne (extra points for attaching a handmade label), cute straw, drink umbrella, party necklace, streamers, party poppers, balloons, candles, and novelty toys. Add a link to an online prerecorded video message. This party-in-a-box is fantastic for expats who are living away from their loved ones.

HELLO
SANDWICH
*
creative
collaborations

Writing my blog has led to me working with some dream partners.

Isetan workshop

Martha Stewart

mt school

Before moving to Tokyo, I worked at *Vogue* magazines for eleven years. I started part-time at reception and moved through departments over the years. I was also studying at the College of Fine Arts, University of New South Wales, majoring in painting and drawing, and later went on to do an honors degree. I would transform myself from a braided-hair-extension-wearing gothic art student into a kitten-heeled, pretend-posh-accented voice answering the phones at *Vogue* (I am not even kidding!). I cringe when I think back to some of the hideous mistakes I made. When I first started, I didn't even know how to use a scanner! But by the time I handed in my resignation in 2010 to move to Tokyo, I was deputy art director of *Vogue Living* magazine, a role I dearly loved. Leaving that job was one of the hardest things I've ever done, but with the cutoff age for a working visa fast approaching,

it was a case of now or never if I wanted to move to Japan. It is one of the best choices I've ever made.

It brings to mind Steve Jobs' advice about following your heart and having faith that the dots will connect themselves down the track. The work I do now is so strongly informed by the skills I learnt at *Vogue Living*: I am forever grateful for the styling, designing, photoshoot skills, art direction—and, of course, scanning tips—that I was taught along the way.

I've been lucky to have worked on some incredible projects in Japan that I never thought possible. I've art-directed a Japanese magazine–book for Éditions de Paris, and Condé Nast publications flew me to Beijing to consult on art direction for AD China. I even found myself on a private tour of the mt factory in Kurashiki. On the following pages are some of the creative collaborations I'm especially proud of.

CREATIVE COLLABORATIONS
*
workshops

My first workshop at the gorgeous Shibaura House.

I held my first craft workshop in Tokyo at the D ai Y event at Daikanyama's fashionable hotel CLASKA in 2010. It was the first of many. From this date I can't count the number of workshops I've hosted. I've hosted some as "Hello Sandwich" alone and others in collaboration with some wonderful brands.

I host workshops almost every month in Tokyo, from locations such as Shibaura House (a beautiful SANAA architect-designed building) to department stores such as the popular Tokyu Hands or Isetan. I've been invited to host workshops in small villages in the rice fields of Niigata and in tiny seaside villages in Tohoku, which were badly hit by the 2011 earthquake and tsunami disaster. Not only are these workshops an invaluable part of Hello Sandwich, they are also such a wonderful way to meet and create with some of the readers of my blog.

CREATIVE COLLABORATIONS

*

Martha Stewart

dream job!

It's fantastic to be able to live in Tokyo and work in a creative industry. I am currently working with a Japanese company in Tokyo that promotes Martha Stewart Crafts products here. It's a great job because I basically get to play with the products and use them to create craft samples. I also host workshops that teach people how to make craft items using these products. The company has opened up some amazing opportunities for me, such as hosting workshops at incredible department stores across Japan.

Like many good things in life, this connection came about organically when I met a friend of a friend at a picnic in Yoyogi Park. She had heard about my blogging for Martha Stewart USA and invited me to host a workshop for the company: she worked there and at the time they were looking for someone to promote Martha Stewart Crafts in Japan. I also promote their craft products on social media.

It's another sign that if you truly dedicate yourself to doing what you love, good things will come from it.

*

Romance Was Born

My fabric was used for garments in the "Kawaii Hawaii" line.

I was lucky enough to be asked to collaborate on a line called "Kawaii Hawaii" with well-known Australian fashion label Romance Was Born. Anna Plunkett, one half of the design duo and a longtime friend, asked me to create an assortment of paper collages and drawings that would be printed onto fabric and made into garments for the line. The process of seeing my collages turned into clothing was completely fascinating.

COLLAGE FABRIC!

CREATIVE
COLLABORATIONS

*

mt

....

Back in Japan
post-tsunami
for the love
of mt!

Just after the 2011 tsunami and earthquake disaster, mt—my favorite brand of washi tape on earth—invited me to host a workshop as part of their popular "mt school" program.

At the time, I was in Sydney while the radiation scares and earthquake aftershocks settled down. The Australian government's travel website had a "Do Not Travel" warning for Japan. I sat at my mom's table in Annandale preparing the workshop details and my mother was horrified that I wanted to return to Japan.

But it was mt! I had to do it. So I collected enough frequent flyer points to make it back. The flight, usually direct from Sydney to Tokyo, stopped in Hong Kong, where all the Australian staff were replaced with local staff. That was scary, I must admit. I swear I have never seen that flight so empty! No one was traveling to Tokyo. My motto was, "I'm doing this for the love of mt!" During transit, I got to chatting with a Japanese guy, thinking that because he was Japanese, he'd make me feel more comfortable about going back to Tokyo . . . The poor man didn't help AT ALL! He told me he'd been in Sydney trying to get work so he could evacuate his family. Back on the emptiest flight now from Hong Kong to Tokyo and I was still thinking, "I'm doing this for the love of mt!"

Touchdown in Narita: so many emotions. Standing on the platform of the Narita Express, I checked the Australian government's website on my phone and saw that the travel warning for Tokyo had been lifted. Nice timing, Sandwich!

PLACES & GLOSSARY

＊

AUSTRALIA

Annandale, Sydney

Culburra, New South
　Wales south coast

JAPAN

Daikanyama

Hakone

Harajuku

Higashikitazawa

Ishinomaki

Kichijoji

Nakameguro

Narita

Niigata

Nishiogikubo

Shibaura House

Shibuya

Shimokitazawa

Shinjuku

Tohoku

Tokyo Skytree

Yoyogi Park

GLOSSARY OF JAPANESE WORDS

ageru *fry*

ajiwau *taste*

akai *red*

amai *sweet*

bento *lunch box*

ekiben *train station
　lunchbox*

fureru *touch*

furoshiki *wrapping cloth*

hanami *cherry blossom
　viewing party*

itadakimasu *thanks
　for this meal*

izakaya *tavern/
　Japanese pub*

kakigori *shaved ice;
　literally, summer ice*

karai *spicy*

kiiro *yellow*

kiku *hear*

kokeshi *traditional
　wooden craft doll*

kuro *black*

kyukaku *smell*

midori *green*

mikan *mandarin*

miru *see*

miso *soybean paste*

musu *steam*

nigai *bitter*

niru *simmer*

obaachan *grandmother*

obento, see bento

ojiichan *grandfather*

onigiri *rice ball*

osanpo, see sanpo

osozai *side dish*

osusowake *share
　something with those
　close to you*

sanpo *walking*

shinkansen *bullet train*

shiokarai *salty*

shiro *white*

suppai *sour*

suso *hem*

tomodachi *friends*

tsukuru *create*

ume *plum*

umeshu *plum wine*

wakare, see osusowake

yaku *grill*

USEFUL WEBSITES

Amazon
amazon.com

Bento USA
bentousa.com

Confetti System
confettisystem.com

Daiso
daisojapan.com

eBay
ebay.com

Etsy
etsy.com

HAY
hay.dk

Lovestar
lovestar.com.au

Martha Stewart Crafts
simplicity.com/our-brands/martha-stewart-crafts

Paper Source
papersource.com

Present & Correct
presentandcorrect.com

Purl Soho
purlsoho.com

Tokyu Hands
tokyu-hands.co.jp/foreign.html

HELLO TOKYO TEAM

bisaijimasumi.com/
    index02.html
collectingspace.blogspot.jp
endorika.com/gallery
studiomid.wordpress.com
yuriyoshida13-droptokyo.
    tumblr.com

ZINES

fragola-tokyo.com
graceleeillustrator.com
everycopy.com
polkaros.com
leetranlam.com
sophieetchocolat.jp

COLLABORATIONS

romancewasborn.com
masking-tape.jp/en
shibaurahouse.jp
marthastewart.com

OTHER

zinesmate.org
geronimoballoons.com
ccommunee.com
vsco.co
fujifilm.com
lullatone.com
sandiebizyscelebrant.com.au
udagawa-file.com
avril-kyoto.com

PROJECT
INDEX

＊

bold text = cute project

italic text = cute living tip

THANK YOU!

from left: Boco, Bisaiji, David,
Yuri, Kat, Akiko, Rika

Being able to have worked on *Hello Tokyo*, my very first English-language craft/lifestyle book, in Tokyo was an absolute dream come true. From its seedling beginnings to this book sitting in your hands right now, I feel so utterly thankful that I was able to have both this experience and the honor to work with so many brilliant people while making it.

It seems so long ago now, but I can very clearly remember my first editorial meeting with Boco-chan, this book's photographer, who is much more like a best friend than just my photographer. We were looking over my 200-page "book mock-up" and shaking our heads, with Boco-chan saying "There's no way you can do all this in that amount of time." Which is where Kat, my amazing assistant, came into the picture. Her motto was "We got this." Kat's incredible help, can-do-attitude, kind nature, and ability to work out what I needed long before I even knew myself was incredible. There is no way this book could have been completed without her help.

My "beastie," David, not only modeled like a pro but also quietly puttered around the studio in his ever-so-charming manner, making everything he touched look like perfection by adding his unique perspective. Thank you also to David for answering my never-ending "Which one do you like better?" questions. The day he unexpectedly turned up at the studio to help brought me to tears. David is one of the most beautiful human beings on the planet, and the studio was brought to life when he was around.

Thank you to amazing food artist Bisaiji-san, whose work never fails to stun me with its brilliance. Stylist Rika-san, who, although only officially styling on two days of the book shoot, loaned about fourteen giant bags of props to me for the entire duration of the shoot.

Thank you to our amazing models, Yuri-chan and Akiko-chan, for bringing your beauty into the pages of this book.

And Boco-chan. Gosh, I don't even know where to start. I love this lady to bits. Boco-chan was there with me every step of the way through this project. Never in my life have I worked with such a brilliant photographer. Boco-chan knows the "Hello Sandwich look" almost better than I do and added so much more to this book than you could imagine. This would never have been possible without wonderful Boco-chan.

Thanks to my lovely literary agents, Pippa and Grace, from Curtis Brown who put the magic into action.

Thank you to the incredible team at Murdoch Books, in particular my publisher, Diana, and her endless calming and supporting e-mails and phone calls. Madeleine, who is the most accommodating and sweetest designer on earth I've had the honor of working with, and Melody, our editor, who managed to tackle the task of turning my "how to make/instructions" and text into something legible.

Thank you to my dearest friends Grace, Yasu, Luke, James, Mami, Lauren, Jessie, Rhys, and Olivia for being a constant support throughout the entire project and for letting me bounce ideas off them. Thank you also to Mami-chan for lending a hand to make some of the sewing projects.

Thank you always to my incredibly amazing mom, Mama-sando, who provides endless support and inspiration to everything I do. Love you, Mama! And thank you to my late father, who taught me so much, especially about photography and design, and whom I desperately wish I could show this book to.

And for anyone who worked on this book with me, I'll leave you with this Hello Sandwich quote "Can I just see one more option . . ."

BYE BYE SANDWICHES

Editor: Cristina Garces
Production Manager: Kathleen Gaffney
Design Consultant: Ebony Bizys
Designer: Madeleine Kane
Cover Design: Heesang Lee

Library of Congress Control Number: 2016941988

ISBN: 978-1-4197-2395-7

Text © 2017 Ebony Bizys
Design © Murdoch Books
First published in 2015 by Murdoch Books, an imprint of Allen and Unwin

Photography © BOCO 2015
Pages 16–17 photo © Kat Chetram;
Page 209 lower right photo © Emma Byrnes;
Pages 212, 213 photos © Tanja Bruckner

Printed and bound in China
10 9 8 7 6 5 4 3 2 1

Abrams books are available at special discounts when purchased
in quantity for premiums and promotions as well as fundraising or
educational use. Special editions can also be created to specification. For
details, contact specialsales@abramsbooks.com or the address below.

ABRAMS The Art of Books
115 West 18th Street, New York, NY 10011
abramsbooks.com